"By under[...] [...]
behavior and using the gr[...] [...]
and approval you have, you can be a
'better' parent. You can have a 'happy' child.

This is the key to all the recommendations
that I make to parents who consult me
about behavioral difficulties. Although I am a
'child' psychologist, I seldom meet face to face
with the children with whom I am working.
I usually never see the child at all,
although sometimes a mother will bring out a
snapshot and say, 'You must see what Bobby looks
like.' Bobby has never set foot in my office,
yet his mother assures me that his behavior has
shown a marked improvement. Instead of spending
endless hours with Bobby talking about
his behavior, I have taught his mother and
father to be Bobby's teachers and 'therapists.'

. . . The office setting is an artificial one
for a child. The place where he or she
shows behavior problems is at home or school. And
the consequences of behavior occur at home, too,
where the time, attention, and praise for
positive behavior should come from the people
who count most—the parents."

"A worthwhile book for any parent . . . realistic and
workable."

Fort Wayne News-Sentinel

ABOUT THE AUTHOR

Dr. Jacob Azerrad is a clinical psychologist who interned at the Children's Hospital Medical Center in Boston. He was an associate professor in the Department of Pediatrics at the University of Virginia School of Medicine. He has taught at Tufts University School of Medicine, The Massachusetts School of Professional Psychology, and Lesley College in Cambridge, Massachusetts. He is a member of the American Psychological Association, the Association for the Advancement of Behavior Therapy, and is currently in private practice in Lexington, Massachusetts.

Anyone Can Have A Happy Child

THE SIMPLE SECRET OF POSITIVE PARENTING

Jacob Azerrad, Ph.D.

WARNER BOOKS

A Warner Communications Company

WARNER BOOKS EDITION

This Warner Books Edition is published by arrangement with
M. Evans and Company, Inc., 216 East 49th Street,
New York, N.Y. 10017

Cover design by Gene Light
Cover photo by Bob Peterson

Warner Books, Inc., 75 Rockefeller Plaza, New York, N.Y. 10019

Ⓦ A Warner Communications Company

Printed in the United States of America

First Printing: October, 1981

10 9 8 7 6 5 4 3 2

To Suzanne and Jeffrey,
who make it all worthwhile

"*Any new theory first is attacked as absurd; then it is admitted to be true, but obvious and insignificant; finally—it seems to be important, so important that its adversaries claim that they themselves discovered it!—*"

William James

Contents

Anyone Can Have A Happy Child

Preface

I look upon behavior, in its simplest terms, as the individual's attempts to make life more satisfying, to put zip and enjoyment into life in the best way he or she knows. Sometimes, the "best" way the individual knows is an inappropriate way, and the result, very often, is an unhappy person. Other times, an individual's behavior is the kind that draws warmth, caring, and success —things that can mean happiness.

During my fourteen years as a child therapist, working with the families of children who have learned inappropriate behaviors, I have gradually developed the methods described in this book. They help parents become *better* parents by showing them how to teach their children ways to behave that will put them in touch with the multitude of satisfactions our world has to offer. The methods are both effective and easily learned, so much so that it is not uncommon for parents to come to me after only a single session and tell me that the problem we had discussed only the week before is no longer a problem.

Almost invariably they add, ". . . and we haven't done anything differently."

In reality, they have done something differently. It has had a major impact on their child's behavior and feelings, yet it is so simple and so grounded in common sense that it is difficult for parents to believe that they have actually been instrumental in causing a real and lasting change. These methods, too, are not only effective in dealing with the child with problems; they also provide all parents with ways to teach values and the many positive behaviors they want their children to acquire in the process of growing up.

The thinking that forms the basis for the methods described in this book is the result of two convergent influences. My initial training in psychoanalytic theory taught me to look at behavior within the context of the total person, rather than as an isolated component of that person. However, this way of thinking, while providing the attitude with which I deal with children's problems, does not provide effective answers to the question of changing behaviors and feelings. The methods I use, then, derive from the second influence, my behavioral training.

The child who is disruptive and who turns off other children (and parents as well) by his behaviors should not be looked upon as an angry child, but rather as one who is reaching out for human contact (a very important satisfaction); he has learned ways that bring people closer, but in *anger* rather than because they feel warmth and caring toward him. He must first learn behavior that will bring people closer because they care about him, behavior that will bring warmth and *affection*. Then we can help him learn to give up those ways of behaving that bring him the immediate but lesser satisfaction of *attention*. Other children, possibly because of painful past experiences with people, turn inward for their satisfactions. They become withdrawn and isolated; they set up an internal "Disneyland" and escape into a world of fantasy that cuts them off from life's real rewards. They, too, can be taught behaviors that draw warmth and caring.

Most important for all children, an appropriate repertoire of behaviors helps to build a strong internal foundation for happiness that lasts far beyond childhood through an entire lifetime. This is a sense of self-esteem, feelings of self-worth that parents can nurture and that are the ticket of admission into the world of satisfaction and success.

Sudbury, Massachusetts
1979

Acknowledgments

A great many individuals have helped make this book a reality, among them Dr. Joel Greenspoon, who taught me a new way of looking at behavior; Richard Barrows, who gave me continued encouragement and support by his many sincere positive reinforcers; Anne Borchardt, who initially recognized the merits of the manuscript and provided the impetus toward its final version; and Herb Katz, my publisher, who offered many insightful suggestions in his readings of the manuscript. But most of all I want to thank my editor, Joyce Christmas, who took the manuscript and transformed it into its present very readable and enjoyable form. Barbara Richan provided not only her excellent secretarial skills, but also her ability to turn my typing and illegible handwritten corrections into a readable manuscript. In large measure, I thank my wife, Eleanor, who on many occasions shared her experiences and understanding of behavior with me.

1
Happy Children

All parents want what is best for their children.

They want them to have friends, to do well in school, learn responsibility, be honest, loving, and kind, and think well of themselves. They want their children to be happy.

Parents want these things for their children, no matter what they themselves are like, or what they think their own failings are.

There are no "bad" parents. None of them set out deliberately to harm their child, even if they have problems of their own in dealing with life. Even if they don't think of themselves as "happy" adults, they certainly hope to have "happy" children, with strong values and open to all the satisfactions life has to offer.

How about being "better" parents, then? Parents are constantly seeking advice on how to raise their children. They look for assistance from books and lectures on parenting, and when they come upon behavioral problems they don't know how to deal with, they turn to professionals. More often than not, they aren't any more enlightened than they were before, because most systems for raising children and most theories currently in vogue about human behavior surround the issues with myths and misunderstandings. Nobody tells parents clearly and simply why children behave as they do; no one explains what role parents actually play in bringing them up, giving direction to their behavior, and teaching them what kind of behavior is appropriate and valued.

The fact is, anyone can have a "happy" child—a child whose behavior is positive and who draws all the many satisfactions available in the world to him or her: friendships, self-esteem and the esteem of others, warmth, and caring.

"Happiness" and "unhappiness" aren't easy to define because they're words with many meanings. They're interpretive rather than objective words. We use them to express our interpretation about the *result* of behavior, rather than its cause, and in this lies the key to raising a happy child.

Children's behavior, good or bad, is directly related to the consequences of that behavior. In almost every instance, it is worthwhile for them to behave as they do. As a consequence of their behavior they are rewarded, with time and attention and a heavy degree of parental involvement. It doesn't matter to children whether they're being rewarded for behavior adults think is "bad" or "good." In either case, the rewarded behavior is likely to continue. It's up to parents to be selective about the kind of behavior that receives their attention, because prior to the teen-age years a child's parents are the most influential people in his life.

By understanding the reality of your child's behavior and using the great power of praise and approval you have, you can be a "better" parent. You can have a "happy" child.

This is the key to all the recommendations I make to parents who consult me about behavioral difficulties. Although I am a "child" psychologist, I seldom meet face to face with the children with whom I am working. I usually never see the child at all, although sometimes a mother will bring out a snapshot and say, "You must see what Bobby looks like." Bobby has never set foot in my office, yet his mother assures me that his behavior has shown a marked improvement. Instead of spending endless hours with Bobby talking about his behavior, I have taught his mother and father to be Bobby's teachers and "therapists."

It is a method that works. The principles that I teach parents can be applied by anyone to raising children, and they can help parents help children who have learned negative behaviors (and who are most likely to be "unhappy" children) discover new and more satisfying ways of behaving.

You are your child's best teacher. Bobby, for example, may have trouble making and keeping friends. He may alienate every kid he meets. But he probably isn't aware that he has a problem that needs to be solved. His mother *is*.

Bobby's not going to love a therapist or psychologist; he doesn't *need* or want that person's attention and approval. He wants love and attention from his parents. He usually isn't interested even in talking about his behavior with a therapist. Very likely he's already getting that from Mom and Dad, for whatever good it does. Finally, he isn't interested in wasting play time to visit the office of a man or woman he scarcely knows. He'd rather be spending his time doing something he enjoys.

The office setting is an artificial one for a child. The place where he or she shows behavior problems is at home or school. And the consequences of behavior occur at home, too, where the time, attention, and praise for positive behavior should come from the people who count most—the parents.

LOOKING AT YOUR CHILD WITH NEW EYES

Parents are often surprised that I am able to work with children I seldom meet.

"Don't you really need to see the child?" they ask. "How can you rely on what a mother or father tells you?"

I can rely very much on parental observations *if* the parents learn to look at the reality of the behavior rather than to interpret what a behavior means.

For example, a mother may say that her child is jealous, immature, irresponsible, shy, sad, hyperactive, angry, depressed. The child "hates school" or "doesn't trust me." Any one of these words describing behavior may mean different things to different people.

Exactly what does "jealous" mean to a particular mother of a particular child? It means not just that the child seems to have "feelings" that are jealous, but that she does specific things: "She throws her toys or has a tantrum when I pay attention to the baby."

That is an objective description of a kind of behavior that expresses jealousy. And now the mother understands *actual* behavior she wants to change: no tantrums, no thrown toys.

What does a mother mean by "immature"? She defines it by saying she wants Billy to be more "grown-up." How do these two abstract words translate into concrete actions? She has to look at Billy's specific behavior to determine what she means by "immature" and pinpoint actions that are "grown-up."

Billy's eight and he won't tie his shoes, although he knows how. Mother has to do it for him. He needs help getting dressed. He won't pick up after himself when he's asked to. Now it's easy for Mother to see specific manifestations of immaturity she wants to change: she wants him to do things for himself, keep his room neat —in short, do the things that mean "grown-upness."

Being objective about problem behaviors is the first part of learning to look at your child with new eyes. There's a second part, and an even more important one. You must also learn to look at your child with eyes that see the quiet, valuable, and beautiful behaviors that are always there in miniature. They all too often go unnoticed and unencouraged because behavior that usually catches our attention is the kind that makes waves, not the sort we label as "good."

Sometimes a child's efforts to be grown-up and responsible, to show caring, to make friends, to learn new things, are so ordinary to adult eyes and so fleeting that they pass us by and are forgotten the next moment. If the behavior is unnoticed or forgotten, the child has no way of knowing that this is behavior the parents consider valuable and appropriate. This child may repeat the behavior by chance, but isn't likely to repeat it because it's the right way to behave, if it hasn't been encouraged within the home.

If good news all too often means no news, bad news (or bad behavior) gives us something to talk about, and we do. "Bad" behavior seldom passes by without comment.

If Polly sits down to dinner and eats what's in front of her, nobody at the dinner table is going to notice. If Polly dumps her plate on the floor and refuses to eat, she's going to get an immediate response. People are going to pay attention. Yet the very fact of attention encourages Polly to do the same thing at the next meal. Logically, if she was to receive similar attention for cleaning her plate without a fuss, she'd do it regularly.

In the first case, in spite of the attention, she can't be called "happy." In the second, with her parents responding positively to this ordinary, expected, and positive behavior, she is more likely to be.

"WHAT ARE WE DOING WRONG?"

When Johnny's mother looks out the kitchen window on a spring afternoon, she notices that Johnny and Freddy, the boy from next door, are tossing a Frisbee around. Then she sees what she sees too frequently these days: Johnny is insisting that he take a second throw because he didn't like what he did the first time. Freddy protests. They're supposed to be taking turns. Now Johnny becomes angry because he's not going to get his way. It's the last straw for Freddy when Johnny calls him a name and hits him. Freddy picks up his Frisbee and goes home. It happens all the time.

"What am I going to do with the boy?" Johnny's mother says in despair. "He's only nine, but he sure knows how to lose friends—if he manages to make them at all."

When Johnny trails into the house, she sits him down at the kitchen table.

"Johnny, for about the hundredth time, how do you think you're going to have any friends if you don't play fair?"

Johnny shrugs.

"Someday Freddy won't come back at all if you're not nicer. How would you like it if Freddy treated you that way? Doesn't it make you unhappy not to have any friends?"

Johnny admits that he's unhappy. He doesn't know why he behaves that way.

"I wish you'd tell me what's bothering you," his mother says. "Something must be, that you

23

can't get along with other kids. Are you worried about something?"

Johnny's willing to talk about it, but they don't seem to be getting anywhere toward solving his problem. Fifteen or twenty minutes later, Johnny's mother is talked out. Maybe it's done some good. She hopes so, because a nine-year-old who can't get along with other boys his age has a problem.

A couple of days later, Freddy is persuaded to come back to Johnny's house with a couple of other boys for a game of baseball. Mother's watching the game from the window again, and when Freddy pitches a perfect strike to catcher Johnny, Johnny can be heard shouting, "Great pitch!" The game proceeds peacefully, and for once there's no trouble.

This day, when Johnny comes in, his mother is busy with something. She doesn't mention the game; after all, it went just the way a baseball game should.

"Who won?" she asks.

"Freddy and I did," Johnny says, and he's sent off to amuse himself until dinnertime. He finds his sister quietly coloring by herself, and ends up pestering her until their mother puts a stop to it.

"Johnny," she says, "what gets into you? You know you're bothering Lisa. Can't you even get along with your own sister? I want you to go to your room and stay there until I call you for dinner. I've had just about enough from you."

Johnny's mother is a kind and caring woman, she doesn't alienate her friends, Lisa gets along well with children, Johnny's father has no trouble getting along with people, yet Johnny has difficulty making and keeping friends. How has he learned this kind of behavior?

"What are we doing wrong?" his parents ask. "Are we bad parents who don't know how to raise our son? Haven't we set a good example?"

Johnny's parents are asking the wrong questions, of themselves and of the child. The questions parents should ask are: What do I see when I look at my child? What do I comment on? What kind of behavior do I encourage?

Johnny in an argument with Freddy? Or Johnny calling out, "Great pitch!"?

Polly refusing to eat her dinner once again and throwing a tantrum when told she has to? Or Polly eating quietly, perhaps agreeing to try a new kind of food, even though she's not sure she's going to like it?

A child who mopes around and claims to be depressed? Or a mostly cheerful child who is "happy"?

Do you see—in a way that really registers in your mind—what is called "bad" behavior, the kind that causes the most turmoil in the family and always gets a response from you? Do you fail to see the good and positive behavior that every child displays at least occasionally, because it is so expected, so ordinary, and so brief that it passes you by and is soon forgotten?

Let's go back for a moment to Freddy and Johnny and his mother.

Johnny's problem behavior with his friend did get a lot of attention. Not only did Freddy go home, but Johnny's mother wasted a good deal of her time talking to her son about it. Those fifteen or twenty minutes they spent discussing what was bothering Johnny to make him behave that way were fifteen or twenty minutes of Mother's undivided attention.

The peaceful baseball game, on the other hand, passed without comment. Johnny's mother didn't do more than acknowledge that it happened. For all practical purposes, she didn't "see" what was going on, although she was watching.

The message to Johnny is clear: negative behavior means attention—all that time and talk, a *response*. There's no reward for behaving well, for doing the things that result in making friends with Freddy and the other boys. He might as well annoy his sister; that's a sure attention-getter.

This simple little scenario isn't rare. You notice disruptive behavior, and you want to stop it, either as it's happening or by getting to the cause so that it won't happen again. Parents resort to a variety of methods to do this. The immediate response is yelling, anger, reprimands, some form of punishment if it's serious enough. Often it means a discussion of the behavior with the child in an effort to get to the reasons why. Then the parents wonder why nothing seems to work, especially when the child turns around the next day and does the very same thing. The result is unhappy children and unhappy parents.

All of these methods for dealing with behavior problems mean that time and attention are being devoted exclusively to the child. And children love attention, never more so than when it comes from those very important people in their lives, their parents. They don't necessarily worry about the nature of the behavior that gets the attention.

What I try to teach parents is that it is just as easy to encourage positive behavior as it is the opposite kind. Attention and encouragement can just as easily be given to "good" (valued) behavior—grown-upness, being a good friend, being responsible, generous, honest, and thoughtful—*if* you learn to see it when it occurs, and *if* you know how to use the power of praise you have as a parent. If you make valued behaviors worthwhile to the child, the child is going to repeat them. As you praise him, you enhance his feelings of self-esteem, and the child begins to feel he is a worthwhile person.

A child who has feelings of self-worth, who cares about himself, is a happy child.

2

Behavior and
Its Consequences

A problem in behavior is not a "thing." Bad behavior is not the surface manifestation of a demon hidden away inside a child that can be exorcised by words, it's not a virus that can be eliminated by a miracle drug, it's not the symptom of a psychological disturbance that traces its origin to some unfortunate event or relationship in the child's life. Behavior, whether positive or negative, is simply the result of the consequences that attend a particular way of acting.

This concept runs counter to the prevailing (and deeply ingrained) belief that the way we behave is caused by something in our minds that controls the way we act.

In 1692 the citizens of Salem, Massachusetts, brought accusations of witchcraft against women, children, and men of the town. Many were executed and tortured to rid them of the demons that inhabited them and endangered the souls of the God-fearing. It was the behavior of the so-called witches that identified them: nine-year-old Elisabeth Parris suffered from fits and had been seen to throw a Bible across the room. Her eleven-year-old cousin, Abigail Williams, tried to run up the chimney and threw firebrands around the house. Other young girls in Salem began having fits and convulsions. Clearly the devil, through the agency of a "witch," a West Indian slave, was controlling the girls, and soon hundreds of others in Salem. The solution was to destroy the demons, a process which, unfortunately, destroyed the human beings as well.

Although the witch-hunting frenzy in Salem passed away, the belief in those demons has managed to survive, in different terms and under new disguises. Today the demon is an "emotional disturbance," a "problem," and while we nowadays don't burn those afflicted with demons, we do put our reliance on equally ineffectual and destructive (at best, nonproductive) ways of removing them. However, just as no one in Salem ever proved the existence of the devil except through the behavior of the witches involved, so are today's demons elusive, except through the behavior that seems to indicate that they are lurking somewhere in the mind. Our form of exorcism is talking about the problem, in the belief that by identifying it, and "understanding" it, it will go away. This procedure is almost as doubtful as burning witches.

When we are talking about behavior, however, we are not talking about our usual concepts of cause and effect, where an outside agent (a "cause," a demon, witchcraft, a psychiatric disturbance) makes a child behave in a certain way (the "effect"). With behavior, cause and effect must be viewed in a different way. It is a parent's ability to see behavior from this new angle that makes it comprehensible: behavior, in the long run, is created by the consequences (attention or lack of it), the *immediate response* to something a child does. A lollipop will stop a temper tantrum; that reward ensures a subsequent tantrum. Praise for a quiet behavior works the same way—only the effect is less noticeable than the silence after tears. But it will occur again, if the reward of praise is there. Not in half an hour, or a day or two, but again eventually.

This way of looking at behavior is quite different from the way in which it is normally viewed. We tend to blame a variety of causes for behavioral difficulties, tracing children's problems to responses to situations over which there is little control: an unhappy relationship between mother and father, for example, the fact that a woman is a working mother, that one child is given less attention than another, or that there is some kind of "emotional disturbance" or "emotional disability." Unquestionably, the way the members of a family relate to each other plays a part in the way a child behaves—but not because the relationships somehow implant the "demon," but in the ways behavior is rewarded or discouraged.

The child who learns to manipulate parents with antagonistic behaviors, and to get attention for guilt-provoking statements such as "You don't love me," is not being driven by demons and/or emotional problems. The child is (when these kinds of statements are habitual) simply seeking—and usually getting—a response: maximum attention and time while the parents try to convince the child that it isn't so. It is not always easy to resist the bait. But while we do need to reassure children in their occasional moments of feeling unloved, parents must respond to the habitual use of attention-demanding behavior with minimum attention and time, and no long discussion to find out *why*, but rather with a clear message that the behavior is disapproved of.

Incidentally, it also isn't logical to attribute good behavior to pure chance (while demons often get the credit for bad behavior, no one suggests that angels are responsible for good behavior). If your child "turns out" well, it is because, consciously or unconsciously, you have given responses—warmth, attention, affection—to positive behavior.

A child who becomes an accomplished piano player, eager to practice and achieve his or her best, doesn't just "happen" to be that way. Somewhere along the line, Mother or Father has given the right encouragement at the right time—immediate, positive consequences for good "piano-playing" behavior. This is like the immediate consequences for early behavior that are so familiar we scarcely view them as similar: the smile and praise for the first word, the first step, the first of all those actions a baby learns as it is growing up. The more positive responses an infant gets, the more likely these behaviors will occur again.

Your child's behavior, all through the early years, is very much in your hands. You need not seek for causes of behavior any further than the way you respond to the child and what you choose to encourage. You have the ability to teach your child the behaviors and feelings that reflect your values and the values you want your child to hold throughout life.

KAREN'S DEMON

Karen is an only child who has many behavioral problems. She would have a hard time in Salem today, let alone three hundred years ago. Her case is instructive, however, because it shows dramatically how different behaviors and their consequences relate to one another. It also shows how parents can take the most difficult situations and, through a step-by-step process, can bring about changes for the better.

When Karen's mother sought professional help from me, she had already seen a variety of therapists who hadn't provided much concrete help in terms of changing Karen's behavior. The list of problems she presented was a long one.

Karen drove away every child who tried to make friends with her to the point that no one ever came around to play with her. She was disobedient to her parents, and she argued just for the sake of disagreeing. She was nagging and persistent to get her own way. She told lies when it suited her, and, most hurtful to her parents, she frequently claimed that they didn't love her at all.

Karen's mother was deeply troubled both by

her daughter's behavior and by the feelings she herself had about Karen.

"You notice she's there, you can't help doing that, and maybe she doesn't bother you at first," her mother said. "But she keeps on and on at you, and after a while you're ready to kill her."

The commonest way to look at Karen's behavioral problems is, of course, to assume that she has an "emotional" problem, a demon which has taken hold in the mind of this seven-year-old and is controlling what she does.

. "I thought I could find out what was causing all this trouble," her mother said. "I've tried to talk to her calmly and sensibly and explain why she shouldn't act this way, and then see if she couldn't tell me what was making her behave this way. I didn't get anyplace."

Karen's mother expressed her thoughts about Karen's behavior in subjective terms, using abstract words that interpreted behavior rather than defined it in concrete terms: lonely, sad, defiant, annoying, dishonest.

The first question that a parent has to answer, however, to make a beginning in dealing with behavior, is: "Exactly what kind of behavior is represented by all those words?" For example, what does Karen do specifically that turns off other children? What exactly does she do that you, the parent, find persistent and annoying?

"Friends?" her mother said. "Well, she doesn't have many, but when other kids are around she'll change the rules of the game to suit herself. I've seen her do that a lot. And she's bossy, she tells the others what to do, what games they're going to play. She argues with them, and her reaction to anything that doesn't please her is to get angry."

Karen's mother talked about how Karen behaved around her: "Constant talking, anything that comes into her head; if I say white, she says black; nagging until I get so tired I usually give in and let her have her way."

Karen's mother was seeking reasons for her daughter's behavior. There was a need to uncover and understand what was going on in Karen's head that made her such a difficult and clearly unhappy child.

"I've failed in my understanding of Karen," she said. "Her behavior has to *mean* something that I can't see, and someone has to help me find out what's troubling her, the psychological problem, and what is responsible for it."

The failure of understanding exists not in an inability to comprehend what is going on in Karen's mind but in what actually causes behavior—her mother's response. When she began to express the nature of Karen's behavior in concrete terms, the mother began to see what it was specifically she wanted for her: the exact opposite of the way she presently behaves. She wants Karen *not* to be bossy, *not* to disagree repeatedly, *not* to tell lies: in other words, to be friendly, agreeable, honest.

How can Karen be taught to stop one kind of behavior and how can she be encouraged to behave in ways that are positive, that make people want to be with her, that will make her a happy child?

The key to Karen's behavioral problems seems to lie in her relationship with other children. No matter how badly she behaves, she's going to get attention from her parents, who must notice her. If she could learn to make friends with and keep as friends children of her own age, she would have a source of satisfaction that would be a big step in the right direction.

What I heard from Karen's mother was that the parents were putting a lot of energy, attention, and involvement into encouraging the wrong kind of behavior, chiding her for losing friends, talking with her about her behavior, arguing with her. Attention is what she's getting, and Karen doesn't differentiate between attention for good behavior and attention for bad.

To lay Karen's "demons" to rest, her parents were going to have to find ways to encourage only positive behavior. My job as a psychologist was to teach them how to teach Karen new behaviors. If she had learned to behave badly because people paid attention when she did, she could learn to behave well for the same reason. The process is the same, whether you are a parent dealing with a single behavioral problem (as is usually the case) or simply trying to raise your children positively. The principle of behavior resulting from the response it gets holds true whether the behavior is terrible or terrific.

In Karen's case, her mother concentrated on helping make Karen a better friend, the opposite of the kind of behavior that caused so much trouble for her. Karen's mother had to look at her with new eyes that actually saw the occasional and fleeting instances of behavior that could draw other children to her. No child is wholly without such moments, and the challenge to the parent is to notice them and use them.

Karen's mother made a list for a week or two of examples of positive behavior that had to do with making friends. She was so accustomed to seeing only the things that troubled her about Karen that she had to make a real effort to see and remember the positive behaviors as they occurred. After a week, she had noted down a handful of occasions, some of them very brief, that were positive, winning-friends behaviors.

Karen's cousin—not a regular friend, but a girl about the same age—came to visit. Karen let her go first in a game they were playing while the grown-ups talked.

Although Karen's baby cousin probably didn't understand what she was saying, she told him how well he was learning to walk. She also picked up a toy he dropped.

A little girl from next door came by to play dress-up from a box of old clothes. Karen let her wear a big floppy hat that Karen usually claimed for herself.

The next step is to take those glimmers of positive behavior and make them important. The way to do it is through time and attention—and praise. Half an hour or more later, after the girl from next door has gone home, Karen's mother must take her aside and talk about the incident, making it come to life again as vividly as possible.

"When Lucy was here this afternoon, and you

were playing dress-up, you let her wear that big white hat you like so much. That was a nice thing to do. It makes me happy to see you share with Lucy. People like that in a friend."

Immediately and casually, Karen's mother follows her praise with ten minutes of doing something Karen enjoys, as if she had just thought of it: "Let's play a game of Chinese checkers." Suddenly, being nice to Lucy is getting the same kind of attention being nasty to Lucy usually gets. Positive behavior has been made worthwhile.

The change in behavior comes when this process is repeated over and over again: a vivid description even an hour or more after the event, re-creating what Karen did, who was there, what happened, what was said; praise from Mother for the behavior; several minutes of time spent doing something Karen enjoys.

The behavior (being nice to another child) has a good consequence (time and praise from Mother). The behavior is worth repeating. (We will go into the process of using praise to encourage positive behavior in greater detail in a later chapter.)

Karen's behavior in many areas began to improve with her parents' efforts to teach her new ways of acting. It became clear that "emotional problems" were not the source of her difficulties. There was no hypothetical demon controlling her behavior. That she began to make friends had nothing to do with talking about what was troubling her, but rather with her new behavior toward other children. And that she gradually stopped following her mother around with a constant stream of meaningless chatter, disagreeing with her or asking nagging questions, couldn't be traced to having uncovered deep resentments or insecurities but to the far simpler fact that Karen's mother no longer made it worthwhile for Karen to continue to do so. Instead of time and attention given to a statement like "You don't love me," her mother's response was, "Karen, you know I love you. I don't want to discuss it"—minimum time, and a clear message: This kind of behavior is not appropriate.

It takes determination on parents' part not to give in to the temptation to explain, discuss, analyze, when the child is touching sensitive areas. We want to be fair to the child and to ourselves, but it isn't necessary to be fair, to hear Karen's side and to justify her parents' position, since this is what teaches Karen that interrupting or constant talking or claiming Mother doesn't love her pays off.

"I spent a lot of time trying to understand something that wasn't even there," Karen's mother said after she had learned how to teach Karen appropriate ways to behave with her praise and discourage the inappropriate ways. "There was no 'problem' in the way I'd been thinking of it. It wasn't some kind of ailment we needed a miracle cure for."

What *was* there was a kind of behavior, and it existed because of the way Karen's parents had always responded to it. When they learned to respond to other behaviors, less noticeable but more appropriate ways of acting—when they saw Karen with new eyes—Karen's "demons" disappeared. Her parents understood her behavior for what it was: something *they* were, with the best of intentions, teaching their child.

3

The Understanding Parent and Other Myths

"Let's talk about it."
"I want to know how you feel."
"Tell me what's troubling you."
"I'm trying to understand. . . ."

It's debatable whether an adult can really "understand" what's going on in a six-year-old's head, or the mind of a kid who's seven or twelve or a teen-ager. It's even debatable whether there's any point in making the effort. Yet parents today are urged to try to "understand" their children, to look for hidden meanings in their words, to find out what's troubling them, what they're thinking, how they feel about their parents, why they act the way they do, what makes them sad or defiant or happy. By entering into a dialogue with your child, you are supposed to be getting close to the sources of behavior—that demon or the "problem" we talked about earlier. It is suggested that understanding will somehow create a bond of affection between parents and children, a one-way street at best, since there's no requirement that children try to understand their parents in return.

It would be fine for everyone if an exchange of words meant real understanding of behavior. It would be gratifying if an understanding parent were all that a child needed to be happy and well behaved. Unfortunately, today's elevation of "understanding" to the pinnacle of perfect parenting is a myth, engendered by the prevailing idea in psychoanalytic circles that talking about a problem solves it. This idea has put troubled individuals on thousands of analysts' couches for years of talking about their "problems" in the hope that it will bring about a resolution through understanding what the sources of the problems are. So pervasive is this belief that parents assume that it will work with children, whether it's a case of continuing behavioral difficulties or just a single incident.

In a situation as simple as "Susie, why did you pick all of Mrs. Smith's tulips? Didn't you know it was wrong?" the answer is likely to be "I don't know, I just felt like doing it."

In an attempt to understand and to help Susie understand, Mother could easily pursue the subject in order to get to the reasons why Susie would take something that didn't belong to her. It may trouble Susie's mother that this is a sign of dishonesty or insecurity. The mother may believe that if she doesn't get to the bottom of the mental processes that carried Susie over to Mrs. Smith's garden, it will happen again. She'll start taking things from others.

It may indeed happen again, not in spite of Mother's attempts to understand but *because* of them. Susie's mother isn't gaining understanding by talking over the incident; she's teaching Susie that she'll pay attention to her when she takes something from their neighbor's garden without permission. Of course, Susie isn't set on a path to habitual bad behavior by this incident and her mother's response—unless her mother's response is itself habitual.

"Understanding" doesn't provide a solution to situations as simple as Susie's expedition among the tulips or as anxiety-provoking as constant mealtime battles where children refuse to come when they're called, refuse to eat, demand certain kinds of food.

Unless a child is physically ill, there's no reason to understand a refusal to eat. But the need to satisfy hunger is so basic that adults see a mealtime drama as signifying a problem they *have* to understand—for some parents a life-or-death matter.

"Suppertimes are miserable," Andy's parents agreed. "He just won't eat, he claims not to like what is served, and then he sneaks snacks between meals or before bed. We've tried everything, giving him the things he asks for—and then won't eat—trying to persuade him, promising him treats if he will just finish the meal."

His father remarked that he thought Andy was trying to punish his mother for some reason by not eating what she prepared. "The look on his face just seems to be saying he's getting even with us for something. We don't have any idea what we've done to make him feel this way. We've tried to talk to him about it, so we'll be able to understand him."

Seven-year-old Andy isn't about to help his parents "understand." There is nothing to understand, except that he has learned to behave in this way at mealtimes (and he is not starving, because he has his snacks to rely on). And what he has learned—most likely because of inadvertent encouragement from his parents, a father who makes an issue of "cleaning up your plate," a mother who equates enjoyment of food with happiness—is that if he doesn't eat, he'll get a lot of attention from everyone around the table. That is all Andy's parents have to understand. He's not "trying to punish" his mother; he's trying to bring her closer by drawing all her attention to himself. By not eating. It isn't necessary to look further than the behavior itself and the consequences to understand what's going on and how to change it.

Andy's "problem" was solved not by understanding what was or wasn't going on in his mind but by giving him new responses to his behavior and new ways of behaving.

First, Andy was allowed to eat only at mealtimes, with no snacks available between meals or before bed. This gave him the choice of going hungry (unlikely) or eating with the rest of the family.

No special meals just for Andy. Meals were prepared according to the preferences of his mother and father.

When he refused to eat ("I don't like chicken," he said the first day, although chicken was generally something he asked to have made especially for him), nobody except his mother said anything: "That's the meal for tonight." No one asked him to eat, or pleaded with him. The conversation went on around him and had nothing to do with his eating or failure to eat.

The first day, Andy didn't finish his meal within thirty minutes, and his mother wrapped the food and put it into the refrigerator.

"I am putting the food away," she said. "If you want it, you can ask me for it."

The first night was a hungry night for Andy. And it was a time without any attention.

The second night was a repetition of the first, except that he asked for his food a while after dinner. He got it cold: no reheating or special treatment.

By the time Andy got the message and started to eat at dinnertime, his parents were beginning to be convinced that there was nothing for them to "understand."

After a couple of weeks, Andy's parents had all the understanding they needed. They had no more dinner-table dramas with Andy at their center. (Recommendations for a specific case of eating problems are given in the Appendix.)

LETTING IT ALL HANG OUT: THE PERILS OF SELF-EXPRESSION

A favorite myth, along with that of the understanding parent, is the idea that self-analysis and setting all your feelings free is good for you, good for your children.

"Let it all hang out," people say; "say what you feel, and you'll get rid of all those bad feelings." While parents are being "understanding" about their children's problems, they're likely encouraging them to talk about why they're angry or depressed, in the real expectation that the children will become less angry, less depressed.

Wrong! The child who's encouraged to talk about how angry or depressed he is is going to get more angry, more depressed. A good test of the validity of this myth is to think back on times when you've been upset and have found yourself talking about it, thinking about it, telling whoever will listen all about it . . . and getting more and more upset with each telling. It works the same way with children. Blowing off steam is one thing. I don't suggest that anyone hold back on expressing emotions, real anger, real sorrow, real happiness, either parent or child. You have a right to get angry, for example, when your child misbehaves. Children have strong feelings, too. What isn't right is encouraging them to talk about the reasons *why*, over and over again, because you think that's going to help use up those feelings.

Consider this: if it is true that expressing anger and depression freely and endlessly uses them up and makes them go away, why isn't the same true of love? Yet no one claims that the more you express your love and caring, the more likely it is that you will use them all up. We don't have a finite amount of love to spend that when it's gone, it's gone for good. The more love you give, the more you have to give—and the more love you get back.

"HAVE YOU HUGGED YOUR CHILD TODAY?"

I never recommend to any of the parents I work with that they "give their child more love." I never tell Dad to spend more time with his son on a Sunday afternoon. I never suggest that the bumper sticker we see everywhere—"Have you hugged your child today?"—is a prescription to cure anything. Certainly, I don't think any of those things do any harm, but I will never suggest that simply spending more time with a child or giving more love is going to resolve any behavioral problems. Yet the reminder to "give your child more love" is offered all too often as a solution to "problems."

Parents are ready victims of the myths that assure them that:

- A disruptive child will cease to be difficult if he or she gets "more love."
- An irresponsible child, a boy or girl who's dishonest, a kid who's having trouble in school, a boy who has no friends, a girl who's selfish, all will start behaving well if they are hugged more often.
- All a child with problem behavior needs is more time with you.

Fine-sounding words, without any real meaning when it comes to teaching behavior or changing it: empty myths that only mislead.

I think love and hugging and time with a child are fine, but if you want to bring about changes in behavior, if you want to strengthen the bonds of affection between you and your child, you have to know *when* to give love and *how* to give it.

You don't make a show of being loving when a child demands it. The only thing a child learns from this is that demanding behavior brings verbal assurances that the child is loved. *Asking for love* is being encouraged.

Loving your child, however, should not be contingent upon anything. The time you spend shouldn't be a bribe for better behavior. The manifestations of your love ought to be your spontaneous response to lovable behavior.

If, on the other hand, you are trying to solve behavioral problems, you can use that time and love in constructive ways. A child will not "repay" your love by changing his behavior just because you have reassured him of your caring, but he will learn new behavior if your caring is a consequence of positive behavior.

"Love conquers all" is one of the enduring myths of our civilization, but the truth is somewhat more complicated. The bonds of caring and affection between parents and children are built up slowly as behavior and consequences make both parents and children more lovable and more loving.

HONESTY IS THE BEST POLICY:
NEGATIVE LABELS

Our ideas about feelings, letting it all hang out, being honest about our emotions, are somehow bound up with concepts about the therapeutic value of self-expression.

"Be honest." It's certainly a valuable goal, and we do want our children to learn honesty, but the result of being up front about everything seems to me to have little to do with the person you're being "honest" to, and a lot with what this honesty is supposed to do for you—let the inner turmoil out, and all will be well. The bad feelings will go away, you'll be a better person.

How, then, do we convey hard truths to our children? The world out there isn't always going to praise. Very often it will criticize. Shouldn't we prepare our children for that, harden them, in a sense, for what is inevitable?

Say, for example, that you're playing tennis with your son. He's a beginner and he's not very good at the game. You know that praise is what he wants, but his overall game has nothing praiseworthy about it. Can you praise him anyhow? Or should you tell him honestly how bad he is, in the hope that this will give him the incentive to try harder and perhaps help him be better able to face honest criticism from others?

There's the old saying "If you can't say anything good about someone, don't say anything at all." Like a lot of old sayings, it has some truth to it. Just because something is true, it doesn't have to be said, whatever the encouragement for total honesty we hear today. It's not going to do much for you or your child to tell him he's a terrible tennis player. Children believe what they hear about themselves. Praise for a good backhand stroke, a fast serve, will mean something. He recognizes the truth of the praise; he can check the validity of your statement about his backhand with another player or a bystander or the tennis pro.

The problem in recognizing the truth comes with the uncheckable, abstract statements about a child a parent may make. If you tell a child that a fire engine is a spoon, he will think you're being silly. He knows from his own experience that there is a difference between them; what you're saying isn't true. If you label a child with a quality, however honest and true you *believe* it to be, the child is out of the realm of fire engines and spoons and into something more difficult for him to make judgments about, abstract personality traits that aren't tied to concrete objects a child can recognize.

Sam is quiet; he doesn't talk a lot when grown-ups are around. His mother defines this kind of behavior as "shy," and Sam frequently hears her saying, "Oh, Sam's the shy one. . . ." Maybe she even implies that shyness isn't a quality she admires, she'd rather have him be more outgoing like his brother.

Sam believes that he is "shy." But who is to tell him what "shy" really means? Is it bad to be shy or is it possibly good? If his mother says he's shy, it *must* be true.

Comments about your child's self are about

things no one can see: Janet is lazy, David acts like a baby, Sam is shy. It's not a question of fire engines and spoons any longer, things that are consistently given the same labels by everyone. Shyness, laziness, babyishness are interpreted from behavior; not everyone will agree on them. The child cannot check on the validity of these assessments from another source, a grandmother, a friend, a brother or sister, because their definitions may be different. Rather, he will take his parents' words as truth: shy boy, lazy girl, dishonest, irresponsible, plain, or stupid. They become his way of thinking about himself. Repeated criticism destroys a child's feelings of self-worth. Labels given by parents define his self-image. Honesty is not the best policy in the current meaning of the phrase, unless it is measured truth, given for positive behavior.

The fact is, honest praise that encourages feelings of self-worth is the one sure way to provide a young person with a defense against the harsher criticisms of the world. A child with self-esteem knows he's worthwhile.

SETTING A GOOD EXAMPLE: DOES IT WORK?

We are told that if we set a good example for our children, they will follow in our footsteps. This is another myth with a particle of truth and not much else. Children do imitate adults, but setting a good example is not enough. Parents who set an excellent example in terms of responsibility may have children who are irresponsible and extremely dependent. Children from families who are gregarious and outgoing may be isolated and withdrawn. Parents, then, must do more than be good examples for their children. They must encourage behaviors they value, and this encouragement is perhaps more important than any example the parents represent.

This is not to say that children aren't influenced by parental example. The beginnings of various kinds of behaviors are often inspired by parents and other influences around a child in his daily life—other children, teachers, relatives, television. A child very often imitates behavior he sees, because, during the early years especially, a child is eager to learn from the world around him and extremely accepting of what he sees and hears.

Positive "imitated" behaviors must be encouraged, as should those apparently spontaneous moments of behavior we deem valuable: a thoughtful gesture, a step toward being grown-up, an interest in learning. They are delicate seeds of behavior that can be nurtured and helped to grow with the right kind of nourishment—praise and encouragement. They can, however, just as easily be discouraged by a failure to give them a boost.

With praise, behaviors will thrive, even if the parents themselves don't always set a good example. Your child can learn to be responsible and independent even if you at times are not a shining example. Parents who don't care about learning can have children who seek out knowledge—if the right kind of encouragement is there.

Shy adults need not have withdrawn children, if they make an effort to provide sufficient encouragement for the child to make friends.

It all comes down to encouraging the kind of behavior that the parents value, whether it is opposite or identical to the way the parent behaves. What is important is that the significant people in a child's life look for valued behaviors and encourage them. The example you set is less a value or a detriment than how and what you encourage with your time, attention, and praise.

THE CHILD THERAPY HOAX

The prevailing myths about raising children and about human behavior in general play a part in creating children with problems and finally send them to sources of help to change their behavior and feelings. There are ways to help a child learn positive behavior, and I believe the most effective way is that described in the following chapters.

There are also methods in vogue that all too often are ineffective. For example, time and again I meet with parents who have had their children in psychotherapy for two or three years with little or no progress. In some instances, rather than improving, the problem becomes worse.

"Our child was in therapy for years," a parent will tell me, "and I never knew what was going on. We saw so little change in all that time."

At the beginning of psychotherapy, the therapist often makes a point of stressing that the therapy will take a long time. The problem behavior has frequently been there for years; therefore it will take years to understand and change it. The therapy may also take years, the parents are told, because the child's "emotional disturbance" is so serious. It's essential to set up the expectation that therapy will take a long time because changes take place slowly, if at all; and the weekly visits by parents and child may continue for years. Without this expectation established at the outset of treatment, the parents at the end of the first year of therapy, seeing little or no progress, might seek help elsewhere.

When parents ask what is going on behind the doors of the therapist's office, they are told little or just enough to satisfy them. Games are used, so they are told, because the child is often reluctant to talk about problems. It is the rare child, in truth, who is verbal enough and willing to discuss things that are "bothering" him or her with a therapist.

To get behind the child's resistance to talk (which is more likely the lack of awareness that there's a problem to be uncovered), the therapist claims to be learning about the child's problems in more subtle ways—games, drawings, play activities. They're not games at all, the parents are told, but methods that enable the trained therapist to look within the inner recesses of the child's mind and help the child achieve "insight" into his "problem."

I've suggested that discussions of feelings and talk about problems don't appear to help a child learn positive, valuable behaviors even when the conversations take place between child and parents. If the person involved in such discussions is a therapist whom the child knows only through weekly visits, there's not even the bond of caring between them, and the discussions are even less effective.

A basic tenet of both child and adult psychotherapy is that the person in treatment wants, at least on an "unconscious" level, to maintain the status quo. He resists change. When I studied psychoanalytic theory a number of years ago, an analyst giving some of the lectures spent considerable time telling us about his patients who had "failed." It wasn't the analyst who had failed. As he viewed it, the patients had a need to hold on to their illness, their "symptoms." This resistance to treatment was more powerful than any treatment methods the analyst had at his disposal, and therefore the patients "failed."

The games and other activities the child therapist uses are means to circumvent the resistance to change; in fact, anything the child does or says in treatment is grist for the mill (largely because the mill is bare, and there has to be something to talk about for two, three, five years). It has "meaning" that can be related to the child as a person and is somehow related to his "emotional disturbance" or emotional problem. Pictures are analyzed for hidden meanings, games are viewed with this same eye to uncover secrets of the child's personality. Projective tests of questionable worth are supposed to suggest what is going on in the child's mind.

All the myths about dealing with children's problems and behavior at home are repeated in psychotherapy with children.

"Let's talk about it. . . ."

"Tell me what's troubling you. . . ."

"How do you feel about that? . . ."

Since there is no research to indicate that child therapy of this type is effective, there is a good argument for methods that do help a child establish behavior we want to see or that help a child with problem behaviors change for the better in a comparatively short time.

Instead of going over and over and over the bad feelings and the bad behaviors, how much more sensible and productive to dwell on the good, however brief the moment, however expected the behavior, however often it occurs. This philosophy of raising children, of helping them solve behavioral difficulties, treats children as the unique individuals they are, responding to the values of their parents and their environment instead of to "demons" over which we have no control.

4

The Road
to Happiness:
Appropriate Behavior

All parents are aware of their day-to-day responsibilities to their children: to see that they're fed and clothed and educated, kept from harm . . . and happy.

It's not difficult to understand what has to be done to take care of the physical necessities. We recognize dangers, we provide the food and clothing, we have school systems to undertake a good part of our children's education. But happiness? Who can define it, let alone say how to achieve it?

The happy child, as we've said, is one who is in touch with the many satisfactions life has to offer. The road to this happiness for both parents and children is simply one of teaching a child an appropriate behavioral repertoire so that these satisfactions are more readily available. In other words, it's our responsibility as parents to teach children appropriate behavior so that people want to be with them, and so that they are proud of themselves, learn to be grown-up, and, in turn, become responsible people.

What is appropriate behavior?

It's not hard to figure out, because it's the opposite of the "wrong" behavior that everyone notices, the disruptive moments I spoke of earlier that get so much attention and so many futile attempts at "understanding." Because we readily see what's wrong, we don't have much trouble knowing what we think the child should be doing.

Knowing, though, doesn't show you how you can encourage the growth of appropriate behaviors or change the direction of a child's behavior from "bad" to "good," from a source of unhappiness to happiness.

SERMONS NO ONE HEARS

Let's take a child who has problems and see how *not* to teach him appropriate new behaviors, and then how to deal more effectively with the situation. The case of Doug is nothing extraordinary. He's a nice ten-year-old, with many friends. He's good to his younger sister, he helps his parents, he doesn't rock the boat at home. His problem lies in school, and it's enough to cause his parents concern.

MOTHER: Doug's not stupid, we know that, but at school he simply has no motivation or a sense of the satisfaction he could get from doing well.

FATHER: The first we really heard about it was from his teacher. She says he daydreams in class, he's completely disorganized about schoolwork, and he never seems to get his work done. That last paper he brought home . . . even I could see right off that he'd done it just to get it done. It was full of careless mistakes, things I know *he* knows are wrong.

MOTHER: He's forgetful about other things, too. Last week he left his brand-new jacket on the playground. I can't tell you how many times he's lost his mittens or forgotten his coat. Of course, he's always forgetting his homework. . . .

FATHER: We're both very achievement-oriented people, and we put a lot of care and effort into our activities. We'd like our kids to be the same way. His younger sister is different. She works hard at school, yet even when she gets a perfect grade and he's obviously a little jealous of her success, it doesn't seem to have the slightest effect on his own schoolwork.

MOTHER: We've had long talks with Doug about how important achievement is, but he scarcely listens. His father goes off to work every morning reminding him to try to do well that day, pay attention, do his best.

FATHER: Doug's a real good kid, except for this one thing. We don't want him to be held back, but the more we talk to him, the less he seems to listen. He's just as careless as ever, daydreams through the whole day. We've tried to set a good example for him, but that hasn't worked. *What are we doing wrong?*

That's a common enough question for parents like Doug's, who are highly motivated, with praiseworthy goals and an obvious concern for their son. They want him to be happy, they want him to do well, and they don't like the constant nagging and the family friction and unhappiness that are inevitable results.

What are they doing wrong?

They want very much to communicate their values to Doug, especially in the one area of school achievement. Their desire, however, is very much at the mercy of ineffective methods. We won't try to delve here into what set of circumstances has made Doug behave the way he does at school. Sometimes even minor incidents can initiate negative behavior that demands attention—and is repeated. By the time Doug's behavior became what might be called chronic, his parents started a concerted effort to communicate their values:

- By *example* ("We're both very achievement-oriented . . ." "We've tried to set a good example for him . . .").
- By *sermonizing* ("We've had long talks with Doug . . . he scarcely listens . . .") and the *criticism* that's implied at least in those talks (". . . how important achievement is *to us*"; in other words, you're *not* doing something that's important to your parents and they're telling you where you went astray).

Children do learn by example to some extent; they do try to imitate their parents. But in and of itself, communicating your values by example is often not very effective. The old Hollywood cliché about the bad kid from the good family, the good girl whose father is a gangster, has, like all clichés, an element of truth to it. The traditional child therapist who "sets a good example" for the child he is working with has to make the effort for many years before he sees his example take hold, if it ever does. Parents with the patience of a saint may hope that their example will give their children the inspiration to imitate them. If they're lucky, it will. But in something as important as raising a child, we should not rely on luck.

The other obvious way to communicate values is by words. But when you're faced with a behavior problem, those words tend to turn into sermons. A sermon, as we know, is a speech that attempts to make people mend their ways: "You are not living up to my expectations and I want you to change in a particular direction."

No one can prove that the sermons preached in houses of worship week after week for centuries or the revival meetings that repeat the same exhortations over and over again have any permanent and positive effect on the masses of people who are listening.

No one can prove (and many are the parents whose experience disproves it) that the sermons they give to their children on good values and good behavior have much effect on the young listeners.

Words from parents can be very powerful, but not, I'm sorry to say, in the context of the sermon.

Part of the problem with sermonizing is that

it seldom praises. Instead, a sermon generally says:

1. This is what you have done wrong, how you have not measured up, where you have failed; and
2. This is how you might change, make amends.

Put in the context of communicating values to a child, this then reads:

1. This is the behavior I am criticizing.
2. This is the way I want you to behave; this is valuable behavior.

Criticism is unpleasant. No one likes to be criticized, nobody is going to feel good about himself if he's frequently dealt negative comments. It hurts, and no one likes to be hurt, physically or verbally. Although people who attend church or revival meetings may be looking for a direction for their lives, it hurts nonetheless when they are told what they're doing wrong by a clergyman who supposedly speaks with the highest spiritual authority. The child who is given a sermon by his parents, who speak to him with the highest authority he knows, is likewise open to hurt by the criticism in their words. Is it any wonder that the words that follow, that tell him what he should be doing, fall on ears that aren't especially receptive?

The natural response to criticism is anger, and then tuning out the message that's supposed to have a positive influence. The child protects himself from the negative words of the criticism by getting angry with his parents, perhaps by attempting to justify his behavior and thus entering a dialogue (and isn't your reaction to criticism by your peers anger and/or an attempt to defend yourself?), or simply by tuning out the unpleasant words—*and everything that follows them.*

The child isn't listening in order to protect himself from painful criticism. Not listening and learning are incompatible.

A child does *not* learn values by hearing them talked about in an admonitory speech following a pattern of criticism first, message last. Doug might well want to do better in school, but his tuned-out behavior to parents and teacher is not out of the ordinary. He's doing in his way what you or I would do under similar circumstances.

There are some who might resort to various forms of punishment to help communicate values: say, sending a child to his room to think about his misdeeds for thirty minutes. Punishment, sparingly used, has some value in raising children, but I can think of very few boys and girls who will voluntarily subject themselves to thirty minutes (or thirty seconds) of painful reflection. They'll be thinking about something, but not what they did or how they're going to improve.

THE TEACHABLE MOMENT

All this brings us to what method to use to teach values, and when. If you want to teach your child values, to help him learn more appro-

63

priate behavior, the wrong time to do it is after criticism. This is the nonteachable moment, when he will not be listening to you—and won't learn anything.

There is a right time, a time when the child is listening and open to learning from what you say. This is the *teachable moment*, a phrase that has been used before in different contexts but is a perfect description of the one time you can be certain that your words are going to be heard and absorbed.

The teachable moment, which is the key to teaching values and behavior, happens right after you praise a child for something he has done that pleases you, that represents a valued behavior you would like to see repeated and, more than repeated, become a part of his personality.

It is human nature to be a captive and attentive audience while you are hearing sincere words of praise that confirm that you actually are a worthwhile person. While a child may be listening to you at other times, and is capable of learning from what you say, you can be certain of your impact only during the teachable moment.

In talking to Doug about his school behavior, his parents' implied or spoken criticism that prefaces their remarks about how he could improve makes such moments almost valueless for getting across what they're saying. Doug is turned off; he's heard it before anyhow, these reminders of his failings. On the other hand, if Doug does manage to get all his gloves, coats, and boots home, if he does produce a better than usual paper, his parents have an ideal opportunity to make the small events worth doing again. If Doug is praised for these desired but regrettably rare occurrences, he'll be listening: tuned in, not tuned out. The praise sounds good, and whatever else his parents have to say about their values won't pass unheeded: the importance of achievement, how responsible it is for him to take care of his clothes, how grown-up he is to do his schoolwork promptly and well. In the teachable moment, Doug's mother and father can communicate the values they feel are important. Although we have a general consensus about what is good behavior and what is not and what values are significant, it truly is in the hands of parents to encourage the qualities that they personally wish to see in their children. Any parent can learn to communicate values purposefully, instead of at random, simply by knowing when a child will be most receptive. They can teach appropriate behaviors, help a child learn positive behavior, and encourage feelings of self-esteem so essential to the creation of a happy human being.

The teachable moment is a critical time that parents have to learn to use consciously. Of course, this isn't an unfamiliar idea to many parents. We all know people who have no trouble choosing just the right moment for spontaneous praise, and it seems that they naturally follow the methods I teach parents. It is likely that their own upbringing has taught them to see and respond to the quiet moments of behavior we wish to encourage. But anyone can do it, whether you want to change a behavior or nurture the seeds of positive behavior until they are strong enough to stand on their own.

COMMUNICATION OF VALUES

The sequence for communicating values to a child is simple, so simple, in fact, that it quickly becomes a natural way of relating to your children.

1. *Awareness.* Learn to look at your children with new eyes. Learn to see the quiet but positive moment of behavior you wish to encourage. I have never encountered a child, however troublesome his behavior, who was completely without a single redeeming moment of behavior. Most parents can find many, if they will look for them; and having learned to notice them, they can help them flourish.

2. *Praise.* Tell your child that he has done something that pleases you, that he has behaved in a way that is well thought of, not only by you but by his friends and the people in the world outside the home. And praise him specifically. Knowing how to praise is as important as knowing when to praise, and we will go into this question in the next chapter. In this sequence, praise gives you the undivided attention of your child.

3. *The teachable moment.* This is the point when you can communicate values to your child. You can teach your child behaviors that you think are valuable by telling him *why* you are pleased with him, and *why* you think this kind

of behavior is important to you. No one promises an immediate transformation, but just as nagging can gradually destroy bonds of affection, and sermonizing can gradually cause a child to tune out completely, so is the opposite true: single moments of praise, words that tell a child how you want him to behave, become his way of thinking about himself and increase his feelings of self-esteem.

4. *Enjoyable time.* A few minutes of quality time spent doing something a child enjoys is an effective way of making behavior worthwhile and confirming the praise you've just given. It's not a bribe—"If you do this, I'll do that for you"—but a form of attention that is more meaningful than attention given, say, for refusing to eat or throwing a tantrum or any one of the many other disruptive behaviors that engage parents and often lead them down a primrose path of trying to understand what is going on in the child's head.

This sequence to communicate values and teach behavior can be applied in just about every situation in raising a child. It's a positive way to help a child learn behavior and, unlike the extended periods of time required for traditional child therapy, it is an amazingly rapid way to change behavior and feelings—even those that have been occurring for years. Best of all, it is entirely in the parents' hands. They set the goals they want to achieve. They make the judgment about the behavior they think is valuable and what is without value or of lesser value. The decisions are not made by a third party, a therapist or an adviser on parenting, but by the people who are most interested in having the child grow up according to their system of values and behavior.

Children, like anyone else, want to feel good about themselves. They'll quickly begin to behave in ways that bring them praise and the warmth, attention, and caring they want. All you have to do to start on the road to happiness is to catch the moment and make it meaningful with praise—each positive word is a small but significant step on the way.

5

"I Am a Worthwhile Person"

Do you know how to praise your child?

Do you know what the true and far-reaching effect of praise is on the child you are trying to raise in the best way you know how?

We have talked about *when* to praise, when to communicate to your child that behavior is valued. Praise gives the child a positive attitude toward himself that can shape his entire life.

YOU CAN BUILD SELF-ESTEEM

I often come across adults who look upon life as a repeated series of examinations. Their daily life is a never-ending attempt to prove their worth, and it's an attempt that's doomed to failure. Although these feelings may spur them on to success in business, academic, and social situations, no accomplishment seems to increase their feelings of self-worth. The success that's achieved is reached at a very high cost: constant tension, never being able to relax because life is an unceasing struggle to affirm that they're really doing a good job, that they're worthy.

Others may lack even this driving urge to succeed. They downgrade all their accomplishments, nothing is "good enough." It is as if such people are saying to themselves, "Whatever I do is worthless because it is what *I* have done, and *I* am a worthless human being." This is rather like the old Groucho Marx joke that he'd refuse to join any country club that offered him membership because it would prove what low standards they had.

What we see in adults is a way of thinking about the self that has its roots in childhood. If no one helps the child establish the basis for self-esteem, if he's never praised and always criticized, he's going to have some serious doubts about his feelings of self-worth. And as that child grows into adulthood he isn't going to have positive feelings of self-worth either.

Parents have a unique opportunity to encourage positive feelings of self-worth in their children. Their words have enormous impact. Giving a child this sense of self-esteem may, in fact, be the most important responsibility parents have, if they want a happy child—if they want the child to become a happy adult.

Praise—specific praise tied to even small events that a child remembers and to the kinds of action we want to encourage—builds self-esteem and helps the behaviors grow like seedlings in a garden. Each time a child finds himself in similar situations, he knows a little more what sort of behavior is appropriate, what will bring him praise and success.

Eventually, what parents see and praise in

these small quiet moments will become the child's customary behavior—a quality of his personality. These traits, their manifestations in the way the child behaves, are what others in the world see and think are worthy of their praise as well.

Thus, when you compliment a child on being polite or thoughtful, for being grown-up or a good friend, you are offering something that has an effect far more important than just making the child feel good for the moment. Little by little, the words of praise given by parents become part of the way the child thinks about himself or herself as a person:

Others like what I have done; maybe I ought to like myself, too. Maybe I am worthy of my mother's or father's words of praise. Yes, I am worthy.

Maybe I ought to like myself.

I am competent, grown-up, responsible.

I know what I'm doing, and I'm doing a good job.

I am a worthwhile person.

In time to come, even when there's no praise forthcoming in a frequently indifferent world, the feeling that *I am a worthwhile person* is always there.

YOU CAN PRAISE TOO MUCH

If you reward a behavior with praise, one of the most powerful rewards I know of for child or adult, that behavior will occur more often. However, you don't need to praise too much.

Excessive praise discourages the internalization of feelings of self-esteem by causing an over-dependence on external words of approval. You're preparing the child for a world in which praise is not given repeatedly for all things that are praiseworthy, and a world that looks upon too much praise as insincere. The internal feeling of self-esteem makes constant verbal praise unnecessary.

Parents may also mistakenly praise the wrong things. Sandy is eight, and nobody would call her a badly behaved child. She's quiet and polite and goes about her business without ever rocking the boat. Her parents have never had to or wanted to criticize her. Yet Sandy has doubts about her worth as a person. She never feels that she's competent, she doesn't really think she ought to like herself. Sandy is a child who has always been praised—but praised not for positive behaviors but for nonbehavior.

"You're such a good girl, you're so quiet, I didn't even know you were there."

"Quiet as a mouse . . . good as gold."

Sandy is praised for doing nothing, and her parents think of her as a "good" child. That she is, but she's probably going to go through life unsure that she's worth anything except when she's not doing anything at all. Others don't say they like what she's done, but what she hasn't done. Parents sometimes fall into the trap of equating nonbehavior with good behavior.

Traditionally "good" behavior (in little girls, especially) is seen as quiet behavior, whereas physical boisterousness has been commonly associated with boys. It's the boys, then, who get involved in situations that create momentary havoc—"bad" behavior—with praise for quiet behavior overlooked.

Chuck discovers that it's fun to throw stones, and then something gets broken. That doesn't get praise from Mother or Father. It gets a talking to, at the very least. It probably doesn't stop Chuck from throwing stones.

How different it might be, though, if Mother or Father took the fact that Chuck is learning to throw well, praised it as a sign of a grown-up ability, and then suggested that balls are meant to be thrown, not rocks—why not use that throwing skill with a baseball or football instead?

Instead of thinking, "I'm a bad kid because I throw stones and break things," Chuck will think, "I'm competent, I do a good job throwing a ball, my parents praise me . . . and I'm worthy of their praise."

What building self-esteem in children does, in short, is make them take their own worth for granted. They need not waste energy on feelings of self-doubt, but will be able to use their energy to work toward productive goals. And this, I believe, is what makes children "happy."

HOW DO WE KNOW IT WORKS?

The process of praise and building self-esteem and the appropriate behaviors in our children is not necessarily a swift one. A word of praise doesn't alter a child's behavior immediately;

encouragement of quiet behaviors as the child shows them from very early years often doesn't have an instantaneous effect.

As a psychologist who has taught parents how to use this method with their children, I know it happens. But parents must have confidence that a process is going on that they can't see immediately, especially when it concerns qualities like maturity and kindness and responsibility.

But it does work.

Think back to the time your child said his first word.

"Mama . . ."

It was probably a major moment in your life.

"Say it again, say 'Mama.' . . ." And say it for Father, for Grandma, for aunts, uncles, neighbors: attention and, implied in that attention, praise.

How about baby's first steps? More praise. The first anything that shows he's making the transition from helpless infant to child.

Encouragement of one word leads to saying more words. Encouragement of the first step leads to an effort to take more steps—in spite of spills and bumped noses. But what about other achievements, less concrete ones, that are also part of growing up? We unfortunately don't pay similar attention to the flowering of less obvious skills for living: kindness and caring, honesty, a sense of humor, a sensitivity to others, all the things we're really talking about when we examine what we mean by a happy child. Yet if we see that learning to walk and talk, learning to tie shoes and eat properly, can be encouraged by praise and attention, why not the others, even if the occasions for, say, honesty don't happen as often and regularly as the necessity for speaking or tying one's shoes? They do, and you can make it happen.

INSTINCTS AND PARENTS

Talking and walking, you might be saying, are instinctive. Of course, if you mean by that the human ability to walk upright and to make sounds that express something one's thinking. But there are instincts and "instincts," and parents today have been confused by what is called "following your instincts" in raising children. All too many advisers on parenting suggest that whatever you do as a parent is okay; the chances are good that "instinctively" you'll do the right thing. This method has a nice sound, but not much substance. Parenting is not an instinct.

Of course we have instincts, not only our means of moving and the way we use our vocal cords, but also instincts for food, for sex, for activity. It's the variety of choices about how those instincts will be satisfied that distinguishes us from ants and bees, who move, make sounds, eat, reproduce, and go about their business within an extremely limited range. A bee from the East Coast of the United States will behave in the same way on the West Coast, but a child born in America and raised in, say, China is not going to be the same child he would have been had he remained in the United States. The in-

75

stincts will be the same; the way of satisfying them will be different. Behavior in human beings isn't imprinted in the genes the way it is with ants and bees.

"INSTINCTS" ARE ACQUIRED

Parents who "follow their instincts" aren't responding to some deep impulse common to all people; they're answering to aspects of their own behavioral repertoire learned from *their* parents. This is neither good nor bad, but it does take away some of the glamour surrounding the mystique of "following your instincts." The "instincts" we're talking about are ways of behaving that were acquired, the way we acquired food preferences, attitudes about religion, politics, men and women—from the people who raised *us*.

You may not be the kind of person who learned to praise spontaneously, for example, but you can make a conscious effort to do so now, even if it runs counter to your so-called instincts: in other words, what you learned in the past. If, on the other hand, you are a parent who does seem to have an "instinctive" ability to see and understand what ought to be praised, you are probably also a person who experienced praise as a child.

The "instinct" for praise is thus, happily, something you can acquire. We're back now to learning to see your children with new eyes—and responding to what you see, however small, quiet, expected it may be, with encouragement and the knowledge that your words are going to have a profound effect on the behaviors you want to see in your child.

SELECTION AND REJECTION: LOVE CAN MAKE A CHILD UNLOVABLE

Unfortunately, Darwin's theory of natural selection doesn't apply to children's behavior. The fittest (or most appropriate) behavior doesn't necessarily survive while the least-appropriate behavior withers on the vine. Parents must do the selecting and rejecting when it comes to raising children, to choose the behaviors they want to survive and those they'd like to see fade away.

"Following your instincts" is a chancy way of making the right kind of selections. What isn't rejected may well end up as the problem behavior that brings parents to child psychologists. That's an extreme point of view, however; even parents who are highly permissive with themselves do put some reins on their children. There are fairly common ideas of "right" and "wrong" behavior—especially the latter, because it tends to disturb the waters in an obvious way.

You're pretty quickly made aware that Doug isn't doing well in school, that Karen doesn't have any friends, that Chuck throws stones, that your son tells lies or your daughter is always a problem at mealtimes. If it's a question of black and white, you don't have trouble recognizing it, and the problem may be just finding a way to correct what's wrong and nurturing what's right. Selection and rejection are somewhat more difficult in the gray areas (and probably the areas where "instincts" are most likely to go wrong).

We want our children to be happy. We want what's best for them. We want to give them what we think will bring them happiness. Like adults, children use *things* as a measure of happiness, and many are the parents who succumb to requests for this toy seen on television, that kind of candy, all in the name of wanting to make their children happy. Material goods, however, merely symbolize how the impulse for doing "something" for a child with the best of intentions isn't the way to raise a happy child. We can do too much for our children. The South Seas idyll, where food falls from the trees in a benevolent climate, where no effort is necessary to survive, is an illusion. And the idyllic tropical paradise that is invested with all the comforts of a technological society loses some of its natural comforts—the idea of the "good life" as exemplified by Western culture doesn't easily graft onto another. It can cause cultural dislocations that aren't quickly remedied. It can cause unhappiness.

In William Gibson's play *The Miracle Worker,* Annie Sullivan encounters the wild and unmanageable Helen Keller and her mother. Mrs. Keller says, "Like a lost lamb in the parable, I love her all the more." Annie, whose task it is to teach Helen, says, "Mrs. Keller, I don't think Helen's worst handicap is deafness or blindness; I think it is your love and pity. . . . All of you here are so sorry for her, you've kept her like a pet. Why, even a dog you housebreak. . . ."

Love, in short, can make a child unlovable, when it is given for behaviors that you want "instinctively" to say yes to . . . and you should be saying no.

6

How to Praise, When to Praise, What to Praise

Parents praise their children naturally. We hardly think about it, although we do know that praise is good—and for most people, easy. What is best for your child is easy for you as a parent. You'll build self-esteem, the quiet inner feeling of competence that helps determine success in life

You shouldn't, on the other hand, find it nec essary to praise your child seven times a day. In fact, as I have already said, if you praise too much you will discourage the development of what we might call "self-praise," the child's ability to know without being told that he is doing well, and you will encourage overdepen dence on external words of approval.

At first your child needs more words of praise, sincere praise for ordinary behaviors. It isn't long before he needs considerably less praise, since we're attempting to prepare the child for a world in which praise is not given repeatedly for all things that are praiseworthy, but one that looks upon too frequent praise as insincere—the pats on the back don't occur all that often. Once praise has taught a child to take his own worth for granted, wasted energy need not be spent on thoughts and feelings of self-doubt, but can be used to work toward productive goals.

WHAT IS YOUR PRAISE REALLY SAYING?

We've talked a lot about when to praise your child and how to use the teachable moment that follows words of praise to communicate values or teach behavior. But telling a parent to praise a child is like a doctor telling a sick person to take some medicine for what ails him without specifying the name of the medicine, the dosage, the length of time it should be taken. *Medicine*, like *praise*, sounds good, but without a few instructions both prescriptions are equally worthless and potentially harmful.

The directions for giving praise are simple, if you want to encourage appropriate behaviors:

- Be specific.
- Give 100 percent praise.

"You were very good" doesn't tell a child much, although it's clearly praise. "You were very good when you helped your brother read that story. That's being thoughtful and grown-up, I like to see that" tells the child exactly what he's done and why it pleases you.

Often what parents think of as praise is in reality loaded with implied criticism, things they would never say if they remembered to be specific and wholehearted about what they're trying to commend. Since what parents pay the most attention to is behavior that rocks the boat, when a child does behave well "for a change" it's behavior viewed in comparison to what is usual. Almost unconsciously, a parent will offer praise for a brief moment of quiet, positive behavior in exactly the wrong terms—praise that's loaded with subtle criticism. The spoken words are praise, but there's a "real" meaning underlying them that children are quick to pick up. The praise is valueless unless it is complete praise, tied to the specific behavior you want to encourage.

Here are some examples of "praise" that's really criticism, and how better the incident might be praised.

Non-praise: You played very nicely this afternoon for a change.

Real meaning: I didn't notice what you did that was so nice, I'm just happy you didn't fight and argue the way you usually do.

"Playing nicely" doesn't say much to a child, and moreover, "for a change" isn't praise at all but an implied criticism of usual behavior. The child has no incentive to repeat what was "nice," and basically what he's been told is that not being noticed is what pleases his parent.

Real praise: You played very nicely this afternoon. I liked the way you showed Jeff how to glue the new model airplane together and then paint it. People like friends who are helpful.

———————

Non-praise: It's about time you picked up your room.

Real meaning: You never pick up your room when I ask you to, and it always annoys me. You did it this time, but it probably won't happen again.

It's no praise at all that does no more than comment on the fact that the child has obeyed a request, especially when it doesn't give any reason for the value of doing a chore or what purpose it serves other than getting something done that Mother thinks is necessary. And the implied criticism ("It's about time . . .") means that it probably won't happen again soon, either.

Real praise: You picked up your room. It looks terrific. I like the way you put all your toys together in one place. It pleases me to see you putting your things in order like this.

———————

Non-praise: You have four A's and a B on your report card. That's good, but we've got to get that B up there.

Real meaning: Those four A's are good, but they're not good enough for me. You won't really measure up in my eyes until you get straight A's.

Praise that is contingent upon perfection is without value. No one is perfect, and in spite of some parents' belief that holding up ultimate goals will make a child try harder, it simply confirms the suggestion that he'll never be good enough, no matter what he does.

> *Real praise:* I'm so proud of you for getting four A's on your report card.

> ———————

> *Non-praise:* I'm glad to see you sharing with your brother for a change.
> *Real meaning:* You're a selfish person. It's about time you began sharing.

Children, as has been discussed, believe what they're told about themselves. If you suggest negative qualities, the child will begin to think of himself that way. Tell a child he's selfish often enough, directly or under the guise of "praise," he's going to believe he is selfish. "If that's what they tell me. They must know."

> *Real praise:* I like to see you sharing with your brother. It was very nice of you to let him ride your bicycle this afternoon.

> ———————

> *Non-praise:* It's nice to see you're not acting silly.
> *Real meaning:* You usually act silly. For once you aren't. I haven't bothered to notice what you're doing well, but it's not important, as long as it's not silly.

This kind of comment is so nonspecific, talking about what a child didn't do, that it can't be called a positive reaction to behavior. And since no one bothers to define what "not silly" is, it's difficult for a child to know what ought to be done to earn parents' praise and, more important, *why* that behavior is valued.

> *Real praise:* I was happy to see that you acted in a grown-up way today. You said "Please" and "Thank you" to the people who were visiting. I was very pleased.

It is so important to communicate a specific, positive message. I saw what you did; I was interested in the things that you did, interested enough to take note of exactly what they were; what you did pleased me; what you did is valued behavior.

VIRTUE IS NOT ITS OWN REWARD

I have encountered parents who, for some reason, feel that praise isn't good for a child, or that it's something meant only for very young children. They feel that a child should behave well without encouragement; it's difficult for them to praise, even when it's explained how the system of praise and the teachable moment works. They feel, in a sense, that "virtue is its own reward."

This may be a laudable philosophy, but it lacks validity in terms of raising children, if you understand that behaviors, good and bad, are learned as the child grows up and do not spring from inborn sources within the mind. Not demons, not angels, but encouragement in the form of time and attention for certain kinds of behavior is going to determine how your child acts.

Children need to have someone proud of them before they can develop feelings of self-worth. It's no virtue to behave well in your young years if you don't know that you've done something virtuous. The "reward" for virtue happens when words of external praise gradually become internalized—"I am a worthwhile person."

"But I don't know how to praise," one mother said. "Even when Kevin does something well, and I know it, it sounds fake when I praise him. Maybe it has to do with the way my childhood was. I was never praised."

This same mother admitted that she never really thought much of herself, and agreed that it was worth making the effort to praise Kevin if it would increase his feelings of self-worth.

"It works," she said later. "Kevin's a changed boy." (Kevin had been having trouble getting along with other children, and praise was intended to encourage new winning-friends behaviors.) "I've changed, too," she said. "It's not so hard for me to see the good things he does and to say how much I like to see him behaving that way. I even find myself doing it with his two sisters, who don't have behavior problems, but they really look pleased when I give them a little pat on the back."

Another common enough belief among parents

is that praise simply isn't good for a child, that it will lead to bad behavior rather than good.

"If I say something good, something bad is sure to happen, so, to be safe, I won't say anything at all."

Or: "It's okay to criticize, because things couldn't get worse, and a few hard-hitting words might make them get better."

In the first case, the "Let sleeping dogs lie" myth is close to the idea of praising nonbehavior discussed earlier. It's also related to the idea that some people have that *anything* good has to be paid for, no pleasure without pain. But it's not true that no praise has no effect. No praise means a child who has no guidelines for what his parents think is valuable.

In the second case, the idea that criticism is a valuable way of making a child behave better is probably a harmful way to teach him anything. If praise helps a child develop a positive image of himself as capable and worthwhile, with a strong ability to praise himself, repeated criticism does precisely the opposite. It creates a negative self-image. The words of criticism become the words heard within, an affirmation of worthlessness.

HOWIE'S SELF-IMAGE

Nine-year-old Howie invariably looked at himself negatively. He was well behaved, his parents said, but his poor self-image was clear in the things he said about himself:

"Nothing ever turns out right for me."

"Every time I try to do something, I goof up."

Increasingly, Howie was reluctant to get involved in activities where success wasn't guaranteed. (For example, he took part in the school track program because he was a better runner than many older boys; he didn't swim willingly "because those kids are too good for me.")

"He watches television all the time, he won't take any initiative," his parents said.

You can't fail if you're watching TV; you can't fail if you're passive.

"We try to encourage him to go out and *try*," his father said. "We do praise him, but it doesn't do any good."

Part of Howie's problem, it turned out, was not only that his negative statements about himself were related to his idea of success, doing things perfectly, but also the result of how people tended to respond to his comments. He was praised, as his parents claimed, but in the form of supportive comments that subtly encouraged the negative idea behind his statements. In effect, he got a pep talk for self-critical statements.

"You really did do a good job, Howie. I know you can do it all the time. You're just such a perfectionist. Don't worry so much."

Positive in themselves, his mother's words confirm pretty much what he thinks of himself: the idea of *perfectionist* and the suggestion that, while he should be able to do it right all the time, maybe he won't.

"Even when he feels he's done something that is out of the ordinary," his mother said, "he brushes aside any kind of praise. If we say, 'You did well,' he'll say, 'Big deal,' almost as if he's saying to himself, 'Sure, I did it, but the real me isn't that way.'"

Specific praise that is tied to behaviors that show him taking the initiative, being active even when there's a possibility of failure, is more likely to bypass his feelings of worthlessness. It indicates both that he's done something out of the ordinary and that his parents care enough to pay close attention to what he did. At the same time, the praise ought not to refer to Howie's expressed feelings about himself, that he's not good enough, which would only reward his self-critical statements.

An example of how Howie's parents learned to use praise to define his worth, his grown-upness, and his ability to take an active part in things going on, can be found in one small incident. Howie, his mother and father, and his twelve-year-old sister went out to eat in a restaurant. In the past, when Howie has chosen something and it didn't turn out to be what he thought it should be, he's said, "Oh, I never pick the right thing," or "I'm too dumb to pick something good, you do it." This day, when the waitress came to their table, he gave his order to her, it was something he enjoyed, and the meal went by without incident or comment from Howie.

Later, his mother took him aside and talked about how he'd behaved. On other similar occasions she might have said, "See, you had no trouble picking something you like to eat tonight."

For a child with good feelings about himself it

might be an adequate comment because he already knows how to do "grown-up" things like ordering food without worrying about doing it right. This kind of praise for Howie is too vague and also reminds him that he's done it in a way he thinks is "wrong" on other occasions.

More specific praise might be "I like the way you ordered in the restaurant. It was very grown-up." Still, it doesn't tell Howie anything out of the ordinary about his behavior.

What his mother said was as vivid a re-creation of the scene in the restaurant as she could make it.

"I like the way you ordered in the restaurant. You told the waitress in a very grown-up way that you wanted french fries instead of baked potato. Then you told her what you wanted to drink and what kind of dressing on your salad. I was really proud of you tonight."

Faced with specific and positive praise, Howie's "Yeah, but . . ." doesn't have a place to go. His parents have helped him take one small step toward a better self-image: I did something right, I behaved in a grown-up way, my mother liked the way I acted, *I* should like the way I act.

Howie's parents carried over this kind of praise to everything they noted that showed taking-initiative behaviors, behaviors that shaped his world, and his fear of failure diminished.

BEHAVIOR IN PARTS

Howie, like all children, will inevitably do something that's less than perfect. Parents have to sort out the non-valued behaviors from the ones they wish to encourage. *Bad* doesn't cancel out *good*. Especially when you are trying to teach positive behaviors, you have to acknowledge both good and bad, and not give too much attention to the negative but enough to the positive.

For example, Johnny breaks a window playing ball, and five minutes later he comes into the house and tells his mother, "I was playing baseball and broke the window in the house across the street."

The behavior has two parts:

- Johnny has broken a window.
- He was honest; he told his mother what he'd done.

To encourage honesty and to keep the lines of communication open between parent and child, Johnny's mother may *briefly* reprimand him for breaking the window, to indicate this is not approved behavior. The temptation in a case like this is to make a dramatic scene, reminding Johnny that he's been told a hundred times not to play ball in that part of the yard, that he was careless, that he has no common sense, but this gives too much attention to the incident. His mother should spend much more time with him praising him for being honest about admitting what he'd done, and indicating that this is important to her, a sign of maturity: that honesty is a valued behavior.

If Howie spills his milk after having ordered

well in the restaurant because he was behaving in a silly way, both parts of the behavior have to be viewed in perspective. Howie is still doing something right; something wrong doesn't cancel it out. He still should be praised.

THE POWER OF PRAISE

Praise is one of the most powerful teaching forces parents have at their command. It is a power that everyone can use in their lives to create warmth and caring between people. It works between friends, husbands and wives, employers and employees, and even strangers.

Caring is, in the end, what we want most *from* our children and in those bonds of affection is the happiness we want *for* them.

The purpose of praise and its effects are three-fold:

- Praise makes it more likely that the praised behavior will occur more often in the future.
- Praise increases the child's feelings of self-esteem.
- Praise increases the bonds of affection between parent and child.

A few appropriate words spoken at the right time can have a strong immediate impact and a long-range effect that endures long beyond childhood.

7

Games Children Play

The value of praise—the right kind of praise at the right time—in raising children positively can't be emphasized too much. Praise itself is a positive action, a giving rather than a taking away, encouragement rather than detraction.

Saying yes to your children is a far happier method of raising them than a constant no—all the negative aspects of criticism and sermons and energy wasted on what they've done wrong instead of what they do that's right and ought to be repeated. Yet as children acquire a growing repertoire of appropriate behaviors, they will test the limits of what they are allowed to do, and if parents don't see this clearly, they can find themselves involved in games of behavior that often carry a large dose of guilt because of the emotional content.

The games children play need a no even though the natural instinct is to play along— justify oneself, in effect, as one would to another adult. A yes to a game a child plays is very much like saying, "Go ahead and say I don't love you, or that you feel depressed, or that you're afraid of things, or that you're stupid, or that you tell lies because you're troubled about something, and I'll feel guilty enough to play along, and spend as much time as I can proving that what you're saying isn't so."

All that time spent is practically an ironclad guarantee that comments like "you don't love me" are going to be a repeated behavior, a permanent game in which both players are losers.

Yet these kinds of behaviors and the testing may have a certain validity in some situations: a child does need to know he's loved; sometimes a complaint is necessary. They need a positive response *from a parent*, not an argument from an adult who's been stung by the suggestion that he somehow hasn't fulfilled his responsibilities.

"YOU DON'T LOVE ME"

Every parent has to deal at one time or another with that sure-fire attention-getter: "You don't love me" (or, equally effective, "You love Mary more than you love me").

The scenario goes something like this:

NINA: You don't love me.

PARENT (protesting, eager to reassure, even guilty): Of course I love you. I love you just as much as I love your sister. Why do you say that? Why do you feel this way?

Several responses like that, and the child will have learned how to get a considerable reward in terms of time and attention, whether or not he actually feels "unloved." Yet the statement deserves an answer, without encouraging a repetition for the wrong (attention-getting) reasons.

Any parent is strongly tempted to respond with assurances, especially when the question of love is repeated: Yes—yes, I love you, yes, you're important, yes, I care about you. But what you have to say, in effect, is: "This is not a question in need of discussion. Of course I love you, and you know it."

Even the child with good feelings of self-esteem is going to say "You don't love me" once in a while. From time to time a boy or girl is going to see a situation where a brother or sister may appear to be favored—a privilege granted for an older child, a surprise gift, anything that doesn't seem "fair." The feeling is often expressed by "You don't love me," meaning, "It's not fair."

The truth is, life isn't especially "fair," in terms of rewards. They don't shower equally on everyone in the world outside the family or even within it. But encouragement of the idea of "You don't love me" by making it an issue to be discussed at length over and over again, just to prove that it isn't true, does a disservice to the child. The protests suggest a possibility that it's true; the question of whether things are "fair" suggests that nothing is fair and everything is open to complaint. I'll talk more about complaining later, in relation to larger problems in behavior, but the matter of love isn't something that needs to be talked about at length.

A child who has feelings of self-esteem that

make him feel worthwhile isn't going to be troubled by day-to-day measurements of rewards and non-rewards as expressions of love. He's already feeling, "I'm okay, I'm competent, I'm as deserving of love as the next person." A moment of doubt is just that, not a way to command attention by saying the one thing that is sure to get total involvement from Mom or Dad.

Learn to say no to the testing, the demand for attention, while still saying yes to the fact of your love. No discussions or explanations, no rewards to prove that you do love your child. Just "You know that's not so. You know I love you." Give assurances of love later for nothing at all, or for following a desired behavior.

Trying to find out *why* you have been accused of withholding your love is not productive. However long you talk, you won't uncover any deep reasons hidden away in the child's psyche. All you're likely to discover is that something happened that didn't fit in with his idea of the way things ought to be.

The way to show a child that you do love him or her is to take the time to say so when the child isn't asking for that reassurance. For example, try saying, "You know, Betty, I really love you" just because you feel like it, for no reason, or because she's done something that's lovable. If you feel guilty about possibly paying more attention to one child and less to another, the time to make up for it isn't when the child confronts you with the thought, but later, in a situation unconnected with the first. You'll avoid the temptation to discuss the issue and you won't plant the idea that a guilt-provoking statement like "You don't love me" is going to be followed by total involvement on your part.

THE FEELING-SORRY SYNDROME

We mentioned earlier Annie Sullivan's comment to Helen Keller's mother about the potential destructive power of too much love and pity. "Feeling sorry" is an adult response, and while some parents feel a sort of formless guilt when a child starts to play the "You don't love me" game, others think the child has good reason for the accusation because of something they've done.

"With the divorce," one parent told me, "we've both been afraid to step too hard on Linda. We give her love to make up for the situation she's in, and we overlook a lot of things. When you say we inadvertently encourage manipulative behaviors, you're right. I let her manipulate me, to make up for the divorce.

"We've heard of cases where divorced couples' kids wind up hating Mother or Father; we're trying to avoid that. So we give in, both of us, to whatever she wants, because we feel guilty about breaking up the family. We want her to love us."

Feeling sorry and guilty is not a sound way to respond to a child's demands. The concern two adults may have about a divorce, for example, or being a working mother and not always available, doesn't mean that a child has a special right to play manipulative games.

Ed is described by his parents as "selfish, only caring about himself and his own feelings." He uses vile language to his parents and friends, and even hits his parents if he doesn't get his own way. His parents view him as a boy "with a lot of hang-ups," and they feel sorry for him because he seems to have "problems."

"I tell him that he is the most important person in the world. I feel so bad for him because he's got so many hangups, so I cater to him. 'Do you want me to get you a pillow? What would you like?' He's just a little kid, after all."

What Linda and Ed have both learned is that it pays to make their parents feel guilty. They have taught them that when they repeatedly make demands, and especially if they suggest they feel unloved, they will get total time and attention. They are being rewarded for making their parents feel guilty, and they continually discover new and better ways to make them feel more guilty.

In the short run, when the parents reassure them, give them what they ask, because they feel sorry, there is brief peace. In the long run, feeling sorry and acting on it, giving the response that's demanded, only means the child will step up the demands. The cycle won't stop; it will continue.

Rewards for asking-for-love behaviors or making-Mother-and-Father-feel-guilty behaviors have one serious consequence: they will make the child unlovable to you and to others. It's a game with no winners at all. We can't give in to guilt; we have to encourage behaviors that don't play on our own hang-ups.

"NOBODY LIKES ME. . . ."

Some children learn to skate, to ride a bike, to cook. Others learn to complain. Complaining is a behavior a child learns like all others, even though it's not necessarily the kind that makes a big splash. Rather, it makes ripples that have a far-reaching effect. The child who's a complainer can turn off friends just as surely as by knocking them down or bossing them around. The complaining child ends up just as "unhappy" as the boy or girl who's not doing well in school, who doesn't get along with other children, or who wages a constant battle of defiance with parents.

Children are adept at the complaining game, although they may be somewhat less subtle than adults. The woman who complains about her husband, the man who complains about his boss, usually has a pretty good story to tell initially—until listeners grow weary of hearing the same litany of wrongs and turn away. Children complain in simpler terms:

"You don't love me, nobody loves me."

"Everybody picks on me."

"I'm stupid."

"My teacher doesn't like me."

"Nobody likes me. . . ."

Parents automatically respond to complaining statements like these with "Yes, I hear the unhappiness behind what you're saying, and I want you to tell me about it." It is as if a complaint signals a basic equation:

A child + a complaint = an unhappy child

and it touches off reassurance responses, understanding, caring, concern, the desire to take away the unhappiness and help the child have good feelings about himself—if only we can find the problem that's causing the unhappiness, talk about it, solve it.

What might begin as a legitimate complaint (kids do pick on other kids, things do happen to make a child feel stupid, a hard-pressed teacher might seem to be unfair) often turns into an effective way of getting attention. The first couple of times deserve to be heard and discussed, but if that doesn't help the complaint, the tenth time won't either. Instead of solving a genuine complaint, parent and child are then giving the complaint problem status in itself, a tale to be told and retold, dissected and put together again. We're back to the myth of "Letting it all hang out," as if talking about "problems" and negative feelings will cause them to disappear.

It is, rather, an occasion to say no, to yourself and the impulse to comfort and reassure, to the child who complains for the attention it gets.

Talking about it won't give you a happy child.

Take, for example, the child who comes home and says to Dad, "I'm stupid."

"No you're not. You're a smart boy. Look at

all the things you can do well, you can build model airplanes, you do well in school, you can play soccer. Why do you feel stupid? Did someone say that to you? Tell me what your problem is. . . ."

The recital of all the things he can do well that prove how smart he is sounds pretty good, and it means a lot of attention from Dad. Let's try it again—soon.

It is much more valuable in terms of discouraging complaining behavior and encouraging a feeling of self-worth to say no: "No, you're not stupid."

Later, when the child has done something that's bright or clever, is the time to tell him he's smart.

"You glued the parts of that ship model very neatly, you're a smart boy. I'm proud of you."

The child has in his hands the well-made ship model, concrete proof that he's not stupid, with the praise and approval that build positive behavior.

"Everybody picks on me."

You can talk about it, with the best intentions in the world, knowing how bad it feels to be picked on or left out, or you can put the complaint in the proper perspective.

"What happened?"

"Well, the other kids wouldn't let me play with them today."

"That's not picking on you. Why didn't they let you play?"

"They already picked teams before I got there."

"Maybe you should get there earlier tomorrow."

Children, like the rest of us, need sympathy and comfort for moments of unhappiness, but too much understanding, too much sympathy, too much effort to turn unhappiness to happiness, almost certainly ensure that the complaint will be repeated.

Unfortunately, the child who learns to complain well, by getting a sympathetic response from parents, is going to turn off other people who don't care whether he's "happy" or not. People outside the family want to be with outgoing, caring people; they want to be with complainers as little as possible. And the loss of the satisfactions that others provide us, the lack of social relationships and caring, truly do make an unhappy person—who now really has something to complain about.

It seems to me that the child who is taught to complain by parents who are concerned about his well-being, who are caring and thoughtful and all too willing to say yes instead of no, is likely to become the adult who scans the world negatively, who is a pessimist, and who is "depressed" because of the limited satisfactions he finds in life.

How much easier for ourselves and our children if they never had the encouragement to complain (in other words, to talk about negative feelings) and to use parents' natural eagerness to have a happy child to establish behavior that almost inevitably means unhappiness.

THE "SIBLING RIVALRY" GAME

Sibling rivalry is a game that may not exist, except in theories and the minds of parents and professionals who have been influenced by them.

Brothers and sisters don't always get along peacefully, and sometimes the conflict is profitable for the attention it creates. If there's a payoff for tormenting a sister or brother, it will continue, but not because of something inborn that makes brothers and sisters natural enemies. Some parents believe in the inevitability of sibling rivalry; they have to accept it and live with it, without understanding that their acceptance encourages the game to be played out to the unhappiness of all.

"Sibling rivalry" is a label that's been attached to a certain kind of behavior the professionals have found fascinating. Since their theories are based on negatives, they haven't come up with a term like "sibling caring." Language plays a big part in determining what we see; we have a label for conflict between brothers and sisters, so we see it and with all good intentions therefore tend to encourage what we see.

Yet sibling caring does exist. Brothers and sisters do care for each other; big sisters take care of the younger children, relationships between sisters and brothers are close and strong through long lifetimes. Girls look up to big brothers, brothers are protective of little sisters. Sibling caring is a real and positive bond, if parents take the time to see it and encourage it. The "game" of sibling rivalry only occurs if the referees—the parents—encourage it because they expect it to be there.

David likes to tease his younger sister. The more he teases her, gets a response from her, and gets a response from their parents, the more he teases. It's not long before it reaches a point where his sister fights back and Mom and Dad step in. They've heard about sibling rivalry, and this must be it—a "problem." The times David has helped his sister read a story, the day he taught her to ride a bike, the time he told her how pretty she looked, the days he's waited to walk her home from school, fade away and are forgotten.

Inadvertently, the observers of the game make it worthwhile by their concern.

Labels influence perception, what we see and what we don't see. People see sibling rivalry, but they don't take time to look for sibling caring. David's parents look for the problem in every situation the two children are together. They step in quickly when he teases or annoys her.

"Leave your sister alone. Why do you bother her? Don't you like her? Are you jealous of her? Don't we treat you both the same way? Do you think we love her more?"

Spoken or unspoken, these questions color the relationship between the children, among all four family members. All in the name of psychological theories that see only the negative, thereby breaking down the bonds of caring between brother and sister instead of building them up.

"NOTICE ME" GAMES: DISHONESTY

Most games aren't played for fun but for the simple goal of getting attention. Some of them, like dishonesty ("He's a born liar . . .") can have present and future consequences that can be very serious indeed. Children aren't "born" dishonest but learn that behavior, often as a way of getting attention.

Dennis, for example, had several brothers and sisters, none of whom were notably dishonest. Dennis, at ten, on the other hand, was a resourceful liar about almost everything. When his mother discussed his behavior and her concern, she couldn't understand why, among her seven children, one was a habitual liar.

"He won't tell the truth if his life depends on it. I'm so busy with all those kids, and they've all turned out well except Dennis."

When she talked more about her children, it was clear that she had only a limited amount of time to spend with each of them. Dennis wanted more time, and got it: by lying frequently and making her spend time trying to figure out whether he was telling the truth about everything—whether he had actually given her back all the change from buying bread, if he had to stay after school, as he claimed, or had actually gone off with his friends without permission.

His "problem," unfortunately, was one that is antithetical to an adult life where honesty is a valuable commodity, not only in dealings with the world in general but in adult personal relationships, where the sense of being able to trust another person's word is extremely important.

The attention-getting game of dishonesty is disturbing to parents, and in Dennis' case, the effort had to be made to see and encourage brief occurrences of a class of behaviors that reflected telling the truth (not easy to uncover if parents have a firm belief that everything a child says is likely to be untrue). But for Dennis there were times when he did give back the right change or when he did tell the truth, and was praised for it. And there were times when he fell into the game but no longer got a more than equal share of his mother's time; instead, the time she gave him was following those behaviors she wanted to encourage.

DEBBIE'S NIGHTMARE: THE FEAR GAME

For weeks, five-year-old Debbie has been waking up screaming every night because of nightmares about "the big germ" and "the terrible lion."

Every night, her parents rush to her bedside to comfort and reassure her that there are no big germs, no lions, that her fears are groundless.

Before bed each night she asks, "Is everything safe?"

"You're safe," her mother tells her. "The shades are all pulled, the doors are locked, we'll leave the night-light on."

The nightmares and fears still come, and during the day Debbie plays "the fear game," discussing her nightmares with her mother and anybody in the family who will listen. Her mother, for her part, sincerely believes that spending time talking will help Debbie let out her feelings about the nightmares and will go a long way toward finding and removing whatever problem is causing them.

By way of these long talks, Debbie's mother, without realizing it and with the best of intentions, is creating a problem rather than solving one. She's telling Debbie that there is a very real payoff for talking about fears, big germs and terrible lions. Not only is she being rewarded by becoming the center of attention day and night, but the more her parents talk about her fears, the more they may be communicating that there may be something to be afraid of.

In effect, Mother is saying, "I am worried about your fears; it worries me so much that I will spend hours with you discussing them. I am fearful, and the thing that makes me so are your big germs and lions."

And Debbie's response is: "If Mother and Father are spending so much time talking about the terrible lion and the big germ, they must also be worried, the lion and germ must be real. If those grown-up people are worried, then I, a little five-year-old, ought to be even more worried."

Because Debbie's parents have effectively said yes to her fears and nightmares, they have found themselves caught up in a perpetual cycle of nightmares and of talk about them that produces more talk, more nightmares, with a handsome reward for Debbie in terms of attention—and frustration, worry, and sleepless nights for her parents.

Behavior like Debbie's has to start somewhere. In her case, we can trace it back to accidental happenings some months before. Debbie had the flu and a high fever. At the time, she talked about bad dreams, and somebody else talked about germs. A little while later, Debbie and her mother talked about a story read at nursery school about "the terrible lion." An older brother and sister teased her, telling her "the terrible lion will get you."

Then, one night, she had a real nightmare featuring big germs and terrible lions, and Debbie found out that her parents' concern, warmth, and caring followed being afraid of nightmares.

Obviously a child who has a nightmare should be comforted and reassured; there is no doubt that parents should be caring. We must, however, make a distinction between comforting a fearful child and going beyond comfort to searching for the root of the problem through long discussions. As soon as parents play psychoanalyst in their well-intentioned attempts to understand the problem, they may be setting up conditions for a relationship between themselves and the child that can be as interminable as analysis itself.

From a molehill they may be creating a mountain. In Debbie's case, her parents, instead of saying no and setting themselves limits in their concern about her fears, have taught her that nightmares and nightmare-related behaviors bring them closer, make them more involved with her.

Those behaviors flourished, beyond Debbie's or her parents' control.

Is it possible to turn her behavior around—in other words, to stop the nightmares?

Yes, if Debbie can be provided with an alternative kind of behavior that also brings her parents close and demonstrates their involvement and caring. She needs to learn those behaviors which will promote emotional growth in place of nightmares, and ways to bring her parents close that also encourage social development and ultimately feelings of self-worth. She has to learn the opposite of being afraid, having nightmares: to have responsible, grown-up behaviors that will get her as much attention as waking up screaming every night.

A NEW WAY OF LOOKING AT DEBBIE

Debbie's parents have been saying yes to behaviors that are immature, dependent, attention-getting, to the exclusion of most others. They have to learn to say no to the game, and find new behaviors to say yes to. They have to learn to look at Debbie with new eyes.

The first step is to note specific examples of grown-upness, of mature, responsible, independent behavior consistent with Debbie's chronological age: for example, such things as getting her own cereal at breakfast time, answering the telephone in a grown-up manner, reading a book by herself, asking for something politely.

These behaviors, whatever their motivation,

are grown-up for a five-year-old, even though they are brief, ordinary, commonplace—she does them all the time.

Once parents have learned how to notice the small, quiet behaviors, they are in a position to use them to teach Debbie ways of bringing Mother and Father closer for positive, grown-up behavior rather than fearful, immature behavior —and to teach themselves new ways of dealing with the nightmares that would not encourage them or ignore them. In short, they learn how to teach their daughter by providing her with a somewhat changed world in which her feelings of self-worth and positive behavior are most important.

Here's a list of grown-up, responsible behaviors that Debbie's parents made note of in one week:

She went upstairs alone to change her dress.
She said "Thank you" when her grandmother gave her a gift.
She helped her mother carry plates and silverware out to the backyard picnic table.
She answered the telephone and took a message from a neighbor for her mother.

Each time Debbie behaved in a positive, grown-up way, her mother or father told her specifically what in her behavior pleased them: what she did, what she said, how she said it that was grown-up—not simply a general comment about acting grown-up.

"It was very grown-up of you to change your clothes by yourself. That pleased me a lot."

"You said thank you so politely to Grandma when she gave you the present. I was proud of you for being so grown-up."

"I like it when you help me set the picnic table like a grown-up."

"You took the message from Mrs. Jones very well, that was very grown-up of you."

The seeds of positive behavior have received an initial push.

An hour or two later, Mother takes Debbie aside and as vividly as possible reminds her of what she did earlier, the grown-up behavior that pleased her.

"You carried all the knives and forks out to the picnic table, like a grown-up person, and it was so helpful to have you set the table with me. You do it very well, and I'm so pleased. . . ."

Immediately and casually, Mother follows her praise with five or ten minutes doing something that Debbie enjoys—reading a story, singing a song together, just having her sit on her lap and talk. Mother doesn't say, "Because you were grown-up, I'll read you a story. . . ." This avoids future bargaining: "Because I did this, you owe me a story."

It is quite amazing to see how quickly specific praise encourages behavior that is grown-up and responsible, as in Debbie's case. The time and attention she gets in this slightly changed world, where she is viewed with new eyes, are as valid to her as the nightmare-induced attention.

Debbie has been given a reason to behave in a positive way . . . but what about the nightmares? It's time now to make an effort to minimize the attention given them.

When Debbie wakes up now, or talks about her fears, her mother listens, expresses a few words of comfort, and that is all. There are no more long discussions about them, no reminders that she has fears ("Did you have a bad dream last night?"), no opportunities to communicate Mother's worries to Debbie. If she's getting the kind of parental involvement she wants from positive behavior and minimal involvement for negative behavior, Debbie isn't going to get so much from nightmares—the "big germ" and the "terrible lion" aren't going to live in her mind the way they have in the past.

Hundreds of cases where parents have learned how to teach their children positive behavior follow the pattern outlined here. We've been talking about games—the testing of how far a child can go to get attention. The system of praise and rewarding with time can be applied to a wide range of behavioral problems that develop, usually inadvertently, when parents allow the negatives to take charge of behavior. But it isn't difficult to see the positive if you look for it, and it's not hard to use the positive to teach your child ways to bring him or her happiness.

8

An Environment with a New Feel

At seven-thirty on a weekday morning, Mrs. Brown is in the kitchen getting breakfast for seven-year-old Gregory and his sister, Pat, who's three years older. They haven't appeared yet, so Mrs. Brown is enjoying a cup of coffee and giving thanks that, so far, the short day has been peaceful. Mr. Brown is out of town on business, as he often is; she doesn't have to leave for her part-time job for several hours.

"Hurry up, you two," she calls upstairs. "You'll be late for school."

Pat joins her, but there's no sign of Gregory. "Where's Greg?"

"Oh, he's fooling around with some stuff in his room," Pat says.

"Get moving, Greg," his mother calls. "Don't forget to make your bed." She assumes he'll refuse as usual.

"I don't feel like it," Gregory says as he puts in an appearance. "You can't make me."

"Don't start," his mother says. "What's bothering you today? You know you're supposed to make the bed."

"I won't. Is that the only jelly doughnut?"

"Yes. You and Pat can split it."

"I don't want to split it, I want the whole thing."

"Gregory," his mother says, "you can't always have it your way. You have to learn to share."

"I don't care," says a furious Gregory. "I want it." He tells her at length why he wants the doughnut.

Mrs. Brown feels her own anger rising. "Look, I don't know what's eating you this morning, but if I hear one more argument from you—"

Gregory doesn't wait. He's out the door, knocking over a chair on his way, with a parting yell, "I hate you."

Pat grabs her books and goes off to school, leaving Mrs. Brown alone to contemplate the scene that has just passed.

Gregory doesn't like her, he won't do anything she asks, he has no idea what it is to be unselfish, his anger at the most trivial things upsets her. At least today they didn't get into the long discussions they usually have. Mrs. Brown tries so hard to understand her son, to figure out what is bothering him that he should always behave this way. She feels it must be that, because she went back to work when he started school a couple of years before, he hasn't gotten the same attention Pat got when she was smaller. She should be able to get to the root of his problem, but it's hopeless. She doesn't understand what's going on in his head, but she's pretty sure she's to blame: Gregory doesn't have any problems at school. His teachers have always found him cooperative and not at all difficult. He seems to take as much pleasure in pleasing them as he does in fighting her.

"I'm convinced he's going to end up as a juvenile delinquent," she says. "His temper is terrible, and I know he thinks I don't care about him. That hurts me so much. I just don't know what I've done to make him this way. Something's bothering him, and somehow it's my fault."

No parent, as we've said, sets out deliberately to harm a child.

Faced with the frustrations of dealing with a child with behavioral problems, such as Gregory's, a parent will say, "I blame myself, it must be something I did to give him a problem. I see what's going on, but I don't understand why. If I understood him, I could help him. I don't, so I can't do anything."

There's one response I have to parents who decide they're to blame for their children's bad behavior and use their guilt and failure to "understand" what's happening to throw up their hands in despair.

I tell such parents, "Go ahead and feel guilty— if you plan every morning all the things you're going to do to make your child unhappy, make him behave badly, make him lose his friends or do poorly in school, cause him to be defiant. Then you have a right to feel guilty. But if you've done what you think is best for your child, and it hasn't worked, there is no reason to feel guilty. Rather, we should look at some better ways of relating to your child."

"We don't try to make our child unhappy,"

every parent will protest. "Still . . . *something* is causing a problem. . . ."

We are back to trying to root out the "demon," the thing that's troubling the child and shows up as surface behavior, the proverbial tip of the iceberg. A crucial point here, I think, is parents' confused idea of what "reality" is. All too many believe that the reality of the situation is the psychological reason behind the behavior. As we have seen, it is all but impossible to uncover any "psychological reasons" for behavior; it is impossible to "understand" in these terms.

The reality, then, has to be the environment in which the behavior takes place, the things that encourage it, good or bad. It's time for parents to take a good long look at what the environment feels like. Is it full of anger and frustrations and sermons about behavior? Or is it one where positive and valued behaviors are recognized and praised?

If you want to feel guilty about your children's behavior, if you want to *understand* in ways that are productive, stop looking for hidden meanings and try to see what's going on right before your eyes. Have you played a part in creating an environment that gives negative behavior room and encouragement to flourish? If you have, take the blame if you wish, and then make the effort to change the cycle of cause and effect, behavior and consequences. Step back and take an objective view of your child's behavior and the environment in which it takes place. Then correct what's not right, by changing the environment and the way behavior is rewarded. This may lack the glamour of profound "psychological" explanations of behavior, but those explanations lead nowhere. We simply have to face reality and reconstruct the environment to give it a positive feeling.

Gregory's mother worries about the reality beneath the surface. She wants to understand.

"He doesn't trust me," she says. "He'll believe anybody, his friends, his grandfather, his sister, his father, before he'll believe what I tell him. It's usually a silly thing, like whether Superman is a real person. I'll say no, it's just a story, and he'll tell me he doesn't believe me, because one of the kids says Superman is real. I want him to think he can trust what I say."

And how does she react when he seems not to "trust" her? When he begins the day with a refusal to make his bed, demands for the whole doughnut, and a furious exit?

"I get angry," she admits. "I've tried talking to him calmly, but he's so stubborn that I get madder and madder and then I end up wanting to strangle him. *I just can't talk to him. I can't find out what's bothering Gregory. He won't share it with me.*"

What does she see?

"I see a very troubled little boy, who no longer knows how to control his temper, who has a lot of resentment against his mother, and who hasn't developed a sense of caring and sharing. I see a problem there that has to be solved if he'd just open up to me."

The pervasive belief that somehow you have to "understand" what's "bothering" a child in order to make sense of his behavior clearly affects the way Gregory's mother looks at him. If only she knew what the problem in Gregory's head was, she'd be able to help him get rid of it. Or would she? Parents seldom go beyond trying to understand the so-called problem to figuring out exactly what is happening, why, and how it can be stopped.

SEEING REALITY

The way Mrs. Brown should be seeing Gregory and his behavior is in terms of the environment in which it takes place: not the tables and chairs and his breakfast and the disputed doughnut, but what is actually going on. This is the way she should learn to *see:*

At seven-thirty she's in the kitchen getting breakfast ready for Gregory and Pat.

Gregory refuses to make his bed, as he always does. This time, though, his mother doesn't argue. There's nothing bothering Greg, except perhaps a dislike of making beds.

"Is that the only jelly doughnut?"

"Yes. You and Pat can split it."

"I want the whole thing."

"Split it or Pat gets it all. Or maybe I'll eat it."

The only problem is just that Greg wouldn't mind having the whole doughnut. And he wouldn't mind getting a lot of attention in the process. He doesn't feel his sister gets more attention than he does, or that his mother doesn't care about him. He's willing to push, though, as far as he can.

"Gregory, I don't want to discuss it anymore. Don't be late for school."

He's out the door, knocking over a chair on his way. "I hate you."

"I'm sorry you do," his mother says. She's done nothing to make him hate her, she is a caring mother. The only thing that's happening is that Gregory would like to have her try to make him change his words.

This is one way of looking at the reality of behavior rather than trying to find out what's "bothering" him. If anyone asked him what was troubling him, he wouldn't have an answer (this gives work to a lot of therapists who spend years trying to uncover the "problem"). The real problem is the child's behavior and what to do about it. He knows if he screams long enough, raises enough confusion, causes his mother anguish and anger, there's a payoff. His environment consists of getting responses, usually negative ones for negative behavior, as in the earlier kitchen scene. He's learned how to behave in that kind of environment. It has nothing to do with what his mother does or doesn't "understand."

If the environment provides equally strong rewards for good behaviors in the same class (say, grown-upness) as for the kind that troubles you, isn't it logical that behavior will change, as rewards for negative behavior are withdrawn? And isn't an atmosphere of trust and closeness and caring preferable to one that just plain feels bad, full of anger and disputes and slammed doors?

Yes. But how do you go about giving the environment a new feel? By eliminating the hostility and defiance and replacing it with conditions that encourage positive behavior.

Gregory's situation is a good example of how a loving mother who cares about her child and wants to see that the child cares for her sets up the conditions for negative behavior. In an effort to "understand," she pays a good deal of attention to the behavior. In a perfectly normal way, she gets angry when her seven-year-old defies her. With good justification, she's upset when he cries and kicks the furniture. Like any mother, she wants him to have what she thinks will make him happy, whether it's the last doughnut or watching the TV show he wants to see. Like every parent, she wants to see that her son trusts her, and sees a refusal to believe her as indicating lack of trust. (Yet those disputes about Superman have nothing to do with "trust" and a lot to do with the fact that time is spent trying to convince Gregory that Mother is right.)

All of these things taken together mean that Gregory is the center of attention in the home environment; the more he is disruptive, the more attention he gets. He's learned to respond in ways that are sure to get total involvement from his mother.

The first step in changing the feel of the environment is for Gregory's mother to put aside her guilt about being the cause of what's bothering him. She didn't do anything intentionally to create his behavioral problems, and feeling guilty solves nothing.

The next step is for Gregory's mother to try to see him with new eyes, to look at his behavior, objectively, and instead of saying that he's self-willed, defiant, untrusting, uncaring, learn to see exactly what he does that is, for example, self-willed and stubborn. This is the specific kind of behavior that ought to be changed. Those new eyes must also learn to see fleeting moments of good behavior. Not simply that "sometimes he's good," but that sometimes "he picks up his clothes when I ask him to"; sometimes "he lets his sister choose the TV program we'll watch"; sometimes "he goes to bed on time."

These examples of what Gregory does that don't make waves in the household—brief, expected, apparently insignificant moments in themselves—are the way to begin to give the environment a new feel. It doesn't matter, either, what the motivation for these small moments was, that he went to bed without an argument simply because he was tired, or that he didn't want to watch TV anyhow, or that for some reason he didn't think twice about picking up his clothes. What matters is that they happened. They are moments of quiet, valued behavior and they ought to be encouraged.

The encouragement comes in the form of a reward, just as bad behavior was rewarded with a powerful response of anger and argument. The reward for positive, nondefiant behavior is praise, along with time and attention. As soon as it starts happening, a little bit of the environment changes; there are moments of feeling good and worthwhile—the teachable moments we talked about earlier, when the child is listening, hearing what you have to say about what pleases you, what you consider valued behavior.

In Gregory's case, the moments of defiance seem to indicate that he's trying to show he's independent and grown-up, although in a negative rather than positive way. "You can't make me" translates into I'm a big boy, I don't have to listen to you." How can his mother encourage him, then, to be independent without the shouting, grown-up without the tears, responsible without the slammed doors?

Gregory's mother has to take note of all those times, however brief, when he does do things that are grown-up and responsible, and then must praise them, make them worthwhile, give him a reason for repeating them rather than the disruptive behaviors that so distress her.

It's easy to make a list, reminders of the ordinary, quiet moments and specific, concrete actions that reflect the kind of behavior parents want to see all the time: behavior that expresses the abstract values this household, these parents, think are important for their children.

So Gregory helped carry the bags of groceries into the house. Why not? He eats here, too. But it's thoughtful and caring, and it doesn't matter that he's really interested in whether Mom bought the kind of ice cream he said he wanted. (Motivation, as has been mentioned, isn't relevant.) It *is* worthwhile making a note of it as something to praise later.

And later, an hour, two, or more, Gregory's mother takes him aside, in private, while his sister is watching TV or doing her homework, and says, "You helped me carry in all those bags of groceries today. That was very thoughtful and grown-up, and it pleased me a lot. I like to see you acting grown-up."

Gregory's mother is labeling his behavior as valuable; she likes seeing him act in a grown-up way, and she's praising him. And Gregory, for that moment, isn't going to respond with "No," or a fit of crying. He's going to listen to those nice words that build up the image of himself as a big boy. (His mother, incidentally, doesn't say something like "It's nice to see you helpful for a change." Gregory doesn't need reminders of his frequent difficult behavior.)

Quickly and casually, Gregory's mother suggests that they do something together that Gregory enjoys, five or ten minutes of talking about something that interests him—his science project, the fortunes of the local big-league baseball team. Or maybe they play a game or look through a catalog of sporting equipment. Enjoyable time with Mother (as compared with those less enjoyable moments when there's defiance on one side and anger on the other and no communication of values at all) creates a totally different atmosphere. The environment does have a new feel to it, and it's surprising how quickly children respond to these new feelings.

Gregory's mother is careful not to say or imply, "Because you were so grown-up, I'll play a game with you." You don't make contracts for good behavior. The reality has to be more subtle; the connection has to be between the action and the praise. The "reward"—the game and the time spent together—reinforces the praise; it doesn't replace it.

If Gregory does voice the idea, "You're playing this game with me because I carried in the groceries," his mother doesn't acknowledge it. She might simply say, "You know, it makes me feel good when you help me."

The fact of praise has been added to a household that had seen little of it, not because Gregory's mother didn't care or didn't want to praise him, but because the environment was such that conflict between mother and son set the tone. It needed some extra effort on his mother's part to see the small moments of quiet, positive behavior that were all too often overshadowed by the battles between them.

There are always three or four or five incidents in the course of a week that reflect the kind of good behavior that ought to be encouraged. The investment in time for praise and a few minutes of enjoyable activity together is quite small. The consequences can be highly gratifying for both parent and child. The child seeks more of those moments that feel good and build self-esteem; the parent is helping to build a new emotional environment that brings the child closer and makes for increased feelings of warmth and affection between parent and child.

It should be emphasized that this method of praise and reward is not, as some have claimed, a manipulative approach to bringing about changes in behavior. It is conscious, of course, whereas the conditions that bring about negative behavior are usually unintentional. Gregory's mother, for example, wasn't aware of the relationship between behavior and consequences—between Gregory's attention-getting tantrums and the time and response she gave them. She was wrapped up in concern about her guilt, his lack of caring, his feeling that she didn't care about him, and on and on. But behavior and consequences can also be viewed in a positive way; the child without behavioral problems has probably been encouraged quite as "unconsciously" by his parents, only in his case the prevailing situation was time and attention for valuable behavior instead of negative behavior.

All this method does is to remind parents of children with behavioral difficulties how to take a step-by-step approach to encourage positive behavior. It's a conscious effort on the parents' part, but just as the child soon learns that he doesn't need constant verbal praise because he knows his parents are aware of what he's doing, so the parents establish a habit of praise and encouragement that becomes almost automatic —no lists, no planned enjoyable time, just spontaneous responses to what the child does that pleases them.

While Gregory's mother is encouraging grown-up behavior and channeling defiance and the desire to be an independent person into positive areas, she also still has to deal with Gregory's tears when he doesn't get his way, the slammed doors, and the arguments. They don't disappear after a couple of weeks of occasional moments of praise, by any means. They still mean attention. But Gregory's mother has to make an effort to minimize attention for negative behavior. She can't continue to let him have his own way, giving in to him when he makes enough noise.

She was always aware that she gave in to him too readily just to keep him quiet. She admitted to trying not to give in to him so often, and her failure meant that Gregory learned that if he kept at her long enough, he'd end up getting his way. If by chance he didn't, he still had the option of screaming and crying—and getting attention when his mother tried to find out what was "bothering" him.

Since Gregory's mother agreed to assume that nothing was "bothering" him, and that a firm refusal to give in to his demands wasn't going to make his hypothetical "problem" any worse and might serve to help change his difficult behavior, it made the effort to say no easier.

"No, you can't have it your way this time, and we're not going to discuss it any further."

Initially, no doubt, Gregory is going to redouble his efforts to get his way. The crying and anger increase for a time. After all, this kind of behavior has always worked before; let's just push it up a notch or two and see what happens. If nothing happens, and at the same time there's a constant stream of praise for what he does that pleases his mother, the negative behavior becomes less and less worthwhile. Of course, it's difficult for a parent who cares to see her child apparently wanting something so much that he reacts in a way we interpret as "unhappy." And of course it's natural for a parent to be angry or annoyed in a head-to-head confrontation with a child who's determined to have his way. But it's worth it to make the refusal to be drawn into a discussion or an argument firm and as brief as possible.

A very real reason why the method of changing a child's behavior described here has proven so effective for preteen-age children is because the environment we are dealing with is a limited one and the primary sources of praise and encouragement are the home and the parents. Outside influences are quite few; parents (and in school, the teachers) have more influence over the quality of the child's environment than they or anyone else will ever have again. Once a child moves into adolescence and adulthood, the outside world, pressure from peers and adults in various roles, broaden the environment so that no one or two persons are in a position to set the tone for environment in quite the same way again.

9
Children Without Friends

Nothing is more worrisome to parents of a growing child than a lack of friends. Why does one child have a knack for driving kids his own age away while another is popular with friends and classmates? Why will one invariably react to other children in ways that are guaranteed to create hostility: being bossy and demanding, starting fights, being selfish? And why do others seem to withdraw into quiet corners and refuse to make any effort at all to involve themselves with other children?

"Don't all kids want friends?" a parent asked me. "Doesn't Billy see that everything he does guarantees that they're never going to come near our house again if they can help it?"

Learning to make friends, even at a very young age, is a behavior like any other. It's taught by having the seeds of making-friends behaviors encouraged, and it flourishes as the satisfactions of having friends provide their own rewards. Unfortunately, the seeds of losing-friends behaviors can also develop if the wrong behavior is encouraged, even in the most inadvertent ways.

Parents can be slow to see the problem developing; it's easier to blame the other kids, to attribute a lack of friends to "shyness," to write off incidents with "Kids will be kids." When it becomes obvious the child simply doesn't have any friends, the first thought parents have is to find some.

"We sent him to camp for a month so he'd make some new friends," a mother said about a boy nobody liked to be with. "He hated it, because nobody wanted to be his friend even there."

Putting a child who drives away friends in touch with other children is not going to bring friends; it will only bring more enemies. A child has to be *taught* how to be a friend.

The parents of ten-year-old Maria said, "She's had more than her share of unhappiness because she's her own worst enemy when it comes to other kids.

"We worry a lot about the things she's always doing that are making her lonely and friendless. She doesn't play well, wants to have it her way. Sometimes she's just plain unpleasant, and it's gotten so that *nobody* will come over here to play, and they certainly don't call her up to play with them.

"We began to think that Maria had some deep psychological problem, because both of us have a lot of friends. We like being with people, and I think they like to be with us. I know Maria is only ten, but I have a picture of her going through life being left out of everything that life has to offer. You know, the girl who is left home on prom night because nobody wanted to ask her out. And then you get to thinking about what you read, the kids who get involved as teenagers with drugs and stuff like that because it's the only way they have of connecting up with other people. Kids like that are losers, and it's upsetting to think of your ten-year-old as a loser already, and you don't know what you did to make it happen.

"It did cross our minds that if only she *acted* differently, she wouldn't have this problem about friends, but what more could we do? We thought we'd raised her properly, and we were completely at a loss about what to do, except take her to a therapist who could find out what was troubling her.

"The therapist told us it might take years to unravel Maria's problems. Well, as far as we were concerned, she didn't have years. We wanted to do something that would work right now, help her to have friends before it was too late."

The method I've described helped Maria build up her winning-friends behavior with praise and encouragement from her parents. It did help her to act differently, just as her parents wanted, and it did, slowly but surely, bring children her own age to her.

"I made a list," her mother said, "noting the times when she did do things that reached out to others in a positive way, and I'm ashamed that I had put so little effort before into seeing the good things about Maria. She's wonderful with her little sister, for example, who's four years younger. Except when she's being stubborn and willful, she *always* says 'Please' and 'Thank you.' I guess it was such expected behavior we never paid much attention. There were other things, too, that we'd never learned to see and encourage. The little boy next door had a broken leg, and Maria was out there the first day he was up, helping him walk on his crutches. I think she was just fascinated by the idea of crutches, but she was pleased when we took her aside later and told her that helping someone like that was what people liked in a friend. And she was out there the next day with him, helping out again.

"Soon after, my sister from out of state came to stay for a couple of days, and brought with her Maria's cousin, who's only a year younger. The two girls seemed to get along well—Maria classified her more as a guest than a playmate at first and behaved well. That gave us a good opportunity to take her aside and express our pleasure at specific things she did with her cousin, and make the connection between that and what people like to see in a friend.

"We kept at it, praise and encouragement and time together with Maria that she enjoyed, and in an amazingly short time we saw a real change in her. She didn't have a whole lot of friends all at once because she'd offended so many of the kids at school and in the neighborhood, but gradually one or two started coming around regularly. What a relief for us and for Maria."

PROMPTING—MORE ENCOURAGEMENT

Maria's parents also helped her strengthen some of the social skills she needed to make and keep friends. They gave her additional supports for her positive behavior through gentle pushes or prompts that helped encourage existing how-to-win-friends behavior and gave her new winning-friends behavior.

Prompts can be useful, but they have to be brief and relatively infrequent so that they don't end up as parental nagging. Once or twice a week, her mother would casually suggest that Maria make some effort to bring friends to her: "Why don't you call up Nancy and have her come over to play Monopoly?" Or "How would you like to have Tina come over to lunch today?"

If Maria failed to take up the suggestion, no more was said about it. If she did respond to the prompt and called the other child, her mother was able to take Maria aside later and remind her of what she had done.

Reminder: "It was nice of you to have Nancy over to play Monopoly."

Praise: "You took turns very well. I like to see you doing things like that, like a good friend."

Enjoyable time: "Let's get out our bikes and take a ride around the neighborhood."

Prompting, if it's gentle, brief, and infrequent, can be an effective way of bringing children together so that someone like Maria will have a chance to use making-friends behavior. Parents are able to see the opportunities and encourage the child to take the initiative with other children.

FRIENDS AND SCHOOL

The one situation when children are most in touch with other children is, of course, at school. On the playground and in the classroom they're interacting with each other for many hours a day, five days a week, and it's here that friends are made or not made. Very often the teacher sees most clearly that a boy or girl is having trouble making or keeping friends. She or he sees the child left alone at recess or being the last one chosen for a team. She sees the classroom behavior that indicates other children don't want to associate with the child. The teacher and the parents can sometimes work together to help a child learn how-to-win-friends behavior and discourage the behaviors that drive other children away.

Eight-year-old Paul, for example, on many occasions shows by his behavior his wish to reach out to other children. Sometimes it's positive and sometimes it's not, and Paul is left in a kind of limbo in relation to other kids.

"He often tries to please his classmates," his teacher says, "but sometimes to the point of going overboard about it. He anticipates other students' needs, offers them pencils and rulers and the like, before they even want them. He's good at math, so he's always offering to help explain math problems."

Yet Paul is a loner; the others don't seek him out.

His teacher: "I've seen him wandering aimlessly around the playground like a lost soul."

His parents: "He just doesn't seem to have many friends; he's a loner."

"That's what's so hard for Paul, I think," his teacher says. "He makes a real effort to reach out to the other kids by offering them assistance and his possessions, and for a minute, maybe, there's some kind of bond between them. Then Paul invariably turns around and blows it. He'll do something that almost guarantees nobody'll be friends with him."

He does things, it turns out, that make people notice him. He's a tattletale, according to his teacher, and she remembers several occasions when he's sparked some kind of conflict with another boy, calling him a show-off because he was walking through the lunchroom with a girl, calling another a dummy because he'd made a mistake in class.

The child who is tattled on by Paul, or the boys who are called names by him, are definitely brought closer to him. *They won't ignore him.* Similarly, the boy or girl whom he helps out with math or who borrows his ruler also isn't ignoring him.

Paul needs to learn new ways of reaching out to children to bring them closer to him, not because they are angry or because of his occasional potentially worthwhile gestures of generosity, but in ways that are enduring and constant.

The primary goal was to help teach Paul those behaviors that make other children want him as a friend: to teach him to break the ice in an assertive way—to reach out and then to learn behaviors that maintain the relationships. His teacher, along with his parents, made the effort, following the method already outlined.

The teacher observed examples of appropriate behavior to be used as the basis for praise and encouragement: however brief, expected, ordinary, whatever the motivation, and no matter what happened before or after. An incident of name-calling, for example, doesn't cancel out an appropriate making-friends behavior before or after it. There were already the occasions when Paul helped with math or shared a pencil; the teacher learned to see others.

"I didn't hear the joke, but Paul responded to something one of the other boys said with a comment that made everyone laugh, really laugh."

In the later moment when the teacher took Paul aside, he was praised for having a good sense of humor, and reminded that people like to have friends who can make them laugh.

"During art activity period, Paul offered a couple of his colored marking pens to a new boy who had just come into the class."

When the teacher praised Paul for being generous, it was also made clear that his behavior to a new student helped to make the boy feel comfortable, and that's a good, making-friends way to act.

The rewards following praise and the communication of values during the teachable moment are, in school, things like carrying a message to the school office, being in charge that day of the classroom plants or animals, being allowed independent activity, or, if the teacher has time, talking about something that interests Paul for several minutes.

At home, Paul's parents, too, followed the method for encouraging making-friends behaviors, and they used prompting as Paul began to respond to praise and reach out in more positive ways to friends. The new boy in school was invited over to play, at Paul's mother's suggestion, and the two boys played happily. Later, she reminded Paul specifically of what they did and how much it pleased her. The praise and the few minutes she and Paul spent together doing something he liked helped build Paul's image of himself as a good friend and made it worthwhile for him to continue to behave in ways that encourage friendships.

"HE'S JUST SHY. . . ."

Norman, on the other hand, could be seen by his teacher as really discouraging friendships. His parents labeled him as "shy." Shy behavior, however, is usually interpreted as rejection by other children; they don't want to be with someone who rejects them.

How did Norman specifically discourage friendships? His teacher was able to make a list of examples.

He kept to himself. For instance, when he came into the classroom he tended not to talk to the other students, kept his head down, was very quiet and nonassertive.

He rejected overtures of friendship. When

Betty offered him her eraser, he said in a very gruff and rejecting way, "I don't need that." When a boy asked Norman if he liked the cartoon he'd drawn, Norman didn't respond at all, as if he simply didn't know what to say in such a situation.

He was sometimes demanding. When his paper blew off his desk, instead of getting it himself, he said, "Get that for me."

For Norman, because he seemed not to know what to say or do in situations that might ordinarily lead to friendship, his teacher (and his parents at home) used gentle prompting to encourage social skills that help make friends.

For example, the teacher made a special effort to say, "Good morning, Norman," when he came into the classroom. It's not likely that a child like Norman (or any child) is always going to imitate the teacher's friendliness, but she can push just a little and say, "Tomorrow when you come into class, when someone says hello, why don't you say hello or good morning back?"

When Betty offers her eraser and Norman says, "I don't need that," the teacher suggests to him how he might respond: "Betty did that because she likes you. Get the eraser from her and say thank you." When the boy asks Norman's opinion of his cartoon and Norman has no reply, the teacher prompts gently, "He likes you, that's why he's asking your opinion."

Later, if Norman follows through on a gentle prompt (and they shouldn't be so frequent that they become aversive; no one likes nagging), teacher or parents have a positive, making-friends behavior to build on, with their praise and encouragement and enjoyable time.

In helping a child learn behavior that brings friends instead of driving other children away, it's important to remember that changed behavior doesn't happen instantaneously. A child isn't going to gather a house full of friends around him overnight. He isn't going to get over being shy right away; he has to learn first, through praise and encouragement, that he's a worthwhile person whom others want to be with.

Negative behaviors don't spring full-blown from the conscious mind of a six-year-old; neither do the kinds of behavior that involve other children. Friendships, even among young people, require small, thoughtful, winning gestures between people to build the bonds of affection and caring. It also takes small negative actions to drive them away. Parents have to be aware of what is happening when they see their children without friends, and once they begin to encourage positive winning-friends behaviors, they have to believe that something is going on quietly, bit by bit, and that it's worth the effort.

Behavior toward friends in childhood is something a person carries through a whole lifetime. Having friends bolsters the idea that "I am a worthwhile person . . . because people out there in the world want to be with me." What a pity if a child is cut off from that kind of satisfaction because caring behaviors aren't given room to grow within the family and without.

"Happiness" for your child isn't a matter of luck, but of being aware of what is going on in the child's life and how his behavior is helping or hindering the image he has of himself, and the image others have.

The child who feels worthless, unpraised, or, worse, heavily criticized may find his satisfactions by withdrawing (being "shy") so that his self-image is protected from further damage.

The child who is aggressive and demanding is going to go through life trying to bring people closer in these inappropriate ways.

The child who has friends is going to feel good about himself—and be a "happy" child. (Recommendations for a specific case of this type are given in the Appendix.)

10

What Does It Mean to Be Grown-up?

"Raising children" is quite a vivid description of what we do as parents: raising them up out of the cradle, so to speak, and pointing them toward adulthood with a repertoire of useful behaviors and social skills, which, for the most part, reflect what we, the parents, believe to be the right ones.

By the time a child has been "raised," it's expected that the child will be an independent individual capable of going out and surviving happily in the world, and will, in turn, most likely want to raise children of his or her own who will become independent human beings capable of finding satisfaction in the world. . . . The march of generations carries the values and attitudes we believe in through the behavior of our offspring and theirs.

Growing up is not an easy process, as any parent knows, but it doesn't need to be full of turmoil and crisis. It's a matter of understanding, defining, and then encouraging what it really means to be grown-up. Since our society has no time-honored "rites of passage" to mark the transition from childhood to adulthood, we tend to define grown-upness in terms of specific privileges (driving a car, wearing makeup, going out on dates, being allowed to vote) or, all too often, in terms of behavior that cannot be called "positive." I think of boys, for example, who define their grown-upness as being hard, violent, destructive, uncaring; of adults who convey their so-called maturity by being sharp operators, authoritarians, cool and detached and cynical. Yet when parents are asked what they wish to see in their children as representative of being grown-up, positive values are stressed: independence, caring, responsibility.

These are the qualities parents want to encourage, in the midst of the other, more negative aspects that seem to define being grown-up. Parents have to *teach* grown-up behavior, the actions that mean independence, caring, and responsibility, and not simply pay lip service to such values.

The seeds of independence exist at a very young age, with the first step a baby takes, for example, with the proud achievement of learning to tie shoes or getting dressed. And these kinds of growing-up, independent behaviors are given praise and encouragement as a matter of course. Unfortunately, in the steps away from total dependence on parents, not all independent behaviors are equally praised, or even recognized. Yet children will grow up and will express their need for independence, often enough in ways that are deemed "bad" behavior.

The road to adulthood isn't always smooth.

The normal and natural efforts of a child to assert independence can come in giant steps, in noticeable positive kinds of behavior, or in small, less noticeable but still positive ways. Or the will to be independent of parents, to be a separate person, can manifest itself in defiance, statements that say, on the surface, "I won't do that, you can't make me"—and mean, "I'm grown-up, you can't tell me what to do anymore."

These kinds of acts of independence are the source of conflict between parents and children to a degree that seems to me unnecessary and unproductive. There's a prevalent way of thinking, that children who defy their parents are "disturbed" by something, that defiance is the symptom of inner problems that have to be uncovered and solved. In truth, however, defiant behavior toward parents and other adults who have some authority over the children is a behavior expressing the need to be separate and independent. The perpetually defiant child is distorting an expression of independence to a point where no one can (or will) ignore it.

"My child is going to be a juvenile delinquent," a parent worries when doors are slammed in anger because a child is defying him or her . . . or when harsh words are exchanged that seem to be saying, "I'm going to have my way, like it or not!" . . . or when strivings to be independent go so far astray that words are replaced by actions that give parents deep concern. Yet, instead of taking steps to diminish the occurrence of distorted expressions of separateness and independence and to encourage positive, grown-up

145

behaviors that more truly express independence, parents center their attention on acts or words that trouble them—and will continue to trouble them, as the child learns the habit of defiance and just what kind of response he can get from it.

"My child is growing up" has subtler feelings behind it for some. A child growing up is a reminder that parents are seeing their own years slip by and, soon enough, the child will be an adult and separate in fact from the parental home. Most parents do want to see their children become mature, responsible adults; their resistance to the inevitable can be made less painful or more fulfilling by seeing that grown-upness is defined in ways that include the real attributes of maturity: responsibility, caring, concern for others, independence, and bonds of enduring affection between parents and children that are not broken simply because a child steps out into the adult world. Part of the role of a parent is just this preparation for adulthood. Yet if we teach our children well, we will not "lose" them.

Still, there are moments of testing, of saying in so many words, "Remember, I'm not a little kid, I'm getting to be grown up." The push and pull in a household as children grow up toward independence can sometimes be horrendous. The point is not to make the defiance worthwhile in terms of its payoff—and extremely damaging in terms of the child's feelings of self-worth and the bonds of caring between parents and child. Nor is the way out to give in to the defiance, which is, in effect, giving the child his own way. We've seen, in the case of Gregory, how at a very young age he had learned to get his own way by pressing the issue to a point where his mother, in despair, let him have it his way. Not just once, unfortunately, but over and over again, until this learned behavior was an ingrained part of him—and required considerable effort to teach him new behaviors.

"I KNOW WHAT'S BEST. . . ."

Taken in themselves, moments of defiance can seem trivial. Parents want one thing: what they think is best for a child. The child wants another, because he or she thinks, "I know what's best. I'm grown-up enough to make my own decisions."

"I want to ride my bike into town to see Joe," a nine-year-old says.

"You can't, it's too dangerous. When you're older—"

"But I know the rules, I'm careful. I am big enough."

Maybe he takes his bike and goes anyhow, which guarantees another unpleasant time when he's found out. Maybe he doesn't go and spends the afternoon in further arguments—the kind of nagging that gets a response: exasperated, angry, impatient, but a response nonetheless.

Kathy says, "I want to spend the five dollars Grandma gave me for my birthday, she said I could."

"You have to save it," Mother says, "or I'll buy something for you with it."

"But it's mine, I'm eight, I know what I want."

"You're not big enough to decide."

Mother thinks she's being reasonable, Kathy thinks she's being treated like a little child. The result is two annoyed people, each determined to have her way, with Kathy more determined than ever to prove she's grown-up. Her way of proof, however, won't necessarily be a positive one, but expressed in terms of defiance.

"Why can't I stay up later? I'm big enough."

"No you're not. You go to bed now."

"I won't, and you can't make me."

Continued discussion, reasoning, or arguing will make defiance at bedtime an expected occurrence, a regular battle, time-consuming and unpleasant.

These are small disputes, with the child trying to exert influence and prove grown-upness in ways that really have nothing to do with being grown-up. If they continue to be replayed day after day, they establish even more negative kinds of behavior that pass for being grown-up and have far-reaching, destructive results. In the cases mentioned, it has to be considered whether it is worthwhile to say no to a child in relation to what he or she is trying to indicate: "I am a grown-up, separate person."

If bike riding really is too dangerous, no is sufficient, for parents have to be concerned about questions of safety. But if he is a careful boy, what is the real value of letting him prove he can go to Joe's house and back safely? Is it really important that Kathy learn saving habits with her birthday gift? Or should she be allowed to show how grown-up she is by choosing something at the store? If it's time to go to bed, then it's time. "You can't make me" deserves no answer, and no arguments. If the child doesn't go to bed, he doesn't, but attention for not going to bed should be minimal.

Twelve-year-old Jerry comes down in the morning, already late for his paper route and too late, he claims, to eat breakfast before he goes out.

"Sit down and eat your breakfast," his father says.

"I don't have time. I'll have some scrambled eggs when I get back if there's time before school."

"You're having your breakfast now, and you're not going to mess up the kitchen again later."

"Oh, Dad, I can't do it. I've got to deliver the papers."

"You should have thought of that when you were lying up there late in bed."

"I just overslept a little, you don't have to keep telling me what to do. . . ."

What Dad is saying to Jerry is, "You're a child, I have to oversee everything you do, and you're going to do things my way."

What Jerry is saying is, "I'm grown-up enough to make my own decisions about when I'm going to eat, and how I'm going to take care of my responsibilities like the paper route."

It's a mild argument, to be sure, but if it happens every day, if no one acknowledges anything about Jerry's abilities to be grown-up and independent, capable of making decisions on his own, Jerry's feelings of self-worth will be diminished. He won't see himself as an independent, worthwhile person, but one who his father thinks can't take anything upon himself While it may be true that Jerry's father is annoyed by his habit of oversleeping and being late for breakfast and the paper route, it's not worth an argument, let alone a battle.

It's worth noting, too, that these kinds of disputes help in the process of developing strong feelings of anger toward the parents who *won't* see a child as grown-up. If the tension continues, Jerry will eventually want to avoid being with his father as much as possible. It's the beginning of a chain reaction, with Jerry's mother being drawn into it on one side or the other, and Jerry himself will be out to prove over and over again in ways that may well be inappropriate that he really is an independent person. In these terms, an "independent" person may be, to Jerry, one who defies his parents and stays out late, or never shows up for meals, or hangs around with kids who define independence in the same ways and get into trouble for it. It's far more productive and valuable to encourage behavior that really is grown-up and independent. It is going to happen anyhow, the fact of growing up, and parents have a responsibility to teach those behaviors that indicate true maturity and responsibility from an early age.

In Jerry's case, both his mother and father must help him learn to feel good about himself as a separate, independent, responsible human being. They have to encourage those behaviors that will confirm to him that he's a grown-up boy capable of making his own decisions about when to eat and when to deliver the papers. His parents have to learn to see the *specific* things Jerry does that show grown-upness and a sense of responsibility, and then encourage that kind of behavior with their praise and approval.

For example, Jerry does get up every morning for his paper route. It doesn't matter that his father says, "I had a paper route when I was a kid, all boys do," or that Jerry does it to earn money to buy a new bike, or for any other motivation. It doesn't matter that he's been doing it for months, and it's so ordinary now that no one thinks twice about it, that it's an expected activity on Jerry's part.

It *does* matter, though, that it's a grown-up and responsible job. Jerry needs to be reminded of that with praise and communication of the idea that taking on a job, handling money, seeing it's done on time, doing it even when the weather's bad or he has something he'd rather do, indicate real maturity.

There are plenty of occasions when the striving to be more grown-up can either be passed over in silence or acknowledged and encouraged. When I've worked with parents about this problem of defiance and shown how it is an expression of a child's wanting to be independent and separate, it's surprising what a list of positive grown-up behaviors they can come up with, things they've learned to see just by paying a little more attention:

Helped his father paint the fence.

Tried eating asparagus for the first time.

Fed the dog.

Closed all the windows during a rainstorm while I was away.

Came home exactly at time promised.

Brought books home from school for a friend who was sick.

Responsible behaviors that young children ought to be praised for; it's a way of teaching them those behaviors you value. And remember this: the child who is made to feel good about himself for behaving in a grown-up and responsible manner is more likely to be the teen-ager out in a much wider world who comes home from dates on time, understands the responsibilities of driving safely, knows how to judge the decisions he or she is called on to make in situations other than the home, reflects the positive values parents have tried to teach rather than the phony separateness and independence that often take the form of defiant behaviors.

Grown-upness, however, is not simply being compliant with parents' wishes. Rewards for being compliant are pretty close to rewards for nonbehavior—the child who is praised for nothing at all: "You're so good, I didn't know you were there." We don't want to teach our children to be robots, nor do we want them to make no waves at all. A human being who simply says yes to everything may have no conflicts, but he will have very few real rewards from life in the outside world.

Teaching independent behavior means that you are giving your child a way of behaving in the world that will enable him or her to deal with the problems and challenges of adolescent and adult life, to be a person less influenced by the pull of others because he has a strong, internal set of values to guide his behavior and help him make his own decisions.

11
Chores Don't Teach Responsibility

How do you teach your child that all-important attribute of maturity, a sense of responsibility?

Being a responsible person is as valued a form of behavior in the adult world as in the life of a family, and the ability to assume responsibility is something that is learned in the process of growing up—if the child is taught how in appropriate ways.

Responsibility and reliability are very often the most noteworthy quality about people one works with or knows on a basis less intimate than friendship.

"He's not a very friendly guy," people will say, "but he does do his job. . . ."

"She's not someone it's easy to get close to, but you can rely on her. . . ."

More often than not, the person who has a sense of responsibility that is recognized by others is someone people like to have around. A person you can trust is a person you want as a friend. The charming, unreliable rogue of fiction and real life is memorable, but few parents want their children to grow up to be like him.

Teaching responsible behavior begins early, like the teaching of other kinds of behavior. "Responsibility," like "happiness," is a word open to many interpretations. It is not compliancy. And it is not simply a question of completing a checklist of tasks, although many parents seem to feel that this is the way to teach responsibility to children.

CHORES AND CONFLICTS

Doing chores—a common enough necessity in many households—is not the way to teach a child how to be responsible, especially if the chore requirement takes on the nature of a battle.

"You're going to do this job whether you like it or not, young man, and you have no choice in the matter" doesn't do much for the relationship between parents and child. The occasion is more likely to be one where the child uses a stubborn refusal to defy his parents and show how independent he is.

I have found, in fact, that parents who have the most behavioral problems with their children are often the ones who give them most chores, the long lists of things to be done at certain times.

"It teaches them responsibility," those parents are quick to protest. "They learn . . . they learn. . . ."

What do they learn? They learn that a parent has decided what chores they are going to do, and if they don't do them, they may be facing a long quarrel, anger, exasperation, even some kind of punishment.

Some of these parents know there's something not quite right about this, that they're asking their children to do chores that they themselves don't especially enjoy doing. Some, although not all, will admit to themselves at least that chores are one way of getting work done. If they have any guilt about giving a lot of chores, they fall back on the "responsibility" argument.

"Everybody has to learn to do things they don't like to do. . . ."

"How else can I teach Lennie responsibility if I don't give chores?"

It is as if washing a floor, taking out the trash, cleaning up a room on a regular schedule, will somehow help prepare a child to become an adult. Yet there are people who as children never made their beds, never mowed a lawn, never dried the dishes, but grew up to be responsible adults.

The result of a program of chores for children who resist the whole idea is children who resent their parents, who get involved in constant disputes about why chores weren't done. There is nothing wrong and there are many things right about a child contributing to the work of the household. Many kids will help spontaneously because they wish to imitate their parents, or because other forms of encouraging responsibility for the well-being of the family give them a push toward less pleasant tasks. If it comes about peacefully, that's wonderful. If, however, in order to have children do their share, you find yourself on a perpetual battlefield, you may be paying too high a price to have clothes hung up, the table set, or the toys returned to their proper place.

The price you may be paying is the immediate stress of making that chore get done and the less-apparent, long-range consequence of raising a child who wants to get as far away from home as soon as possible.

Mrs. Harris talked about the difficulties of her situation, raising five children between the ages of about eleven and nineteen. Mrs. Harris had been widowed a few years earlier, when the youngest boy was about seven, and she had returned to work full-time as a dietician at a local school.

"I have to have the children do chores," she said. "I just don't have the time to do the laundry and the housecleaning, the dishes and the cooking, and work as well. They have to pitch in and help out. Of course, even before their father died, we gave them chores to do. The girls had their jobs to do around the house from the time they were little, and the boys helped out, too. But even then there was never a time when they didn't resist every step of the way. We couldn't seem to make them understand that this was the kind of thing they'd have to do when they were grown-up, so it was good for them to learn to take on responsibilities now.

"Now life is so unpleasant trying to get them to do things. And I feel guilty that they don't have a father and I have to be away so much of the day at work."

Mrs. Harris had lists all over the place, about who should do what when, and she had a constant fight on her hands.

The problem was not that she needed help in running the household and wasn't getting it. The problem was that she was confusing chores with responsibility and paying too high a price in terms of the gradual destruction of the bonds between herself and her children just to get chores done. Doing chores per se is not grown-up behavior, but understanding why chores need to be done is. Mrs. Harris was looking at lists instead of seeing her children.

"I've lost my two oldest girls," she said. "Both of them are engaged or close to it. They're still living at home, but you couldn't guess it from the time they spend there. The people they're close to are their fiancés' families. The younger one even cooks dinner over at their place, and the older of the two is relying on the boy's mother for advice about the wedding."

The three youngest children?

"Well, yes, I still have them doing their chores, and the two big girls, too, when I can get them to."

Any problems with the young ones?

"You know how kids are, it's a constant struggle to get them just to take out the trash and take their proper turns doing dishes. Yes, I guess you could say that getting chores done always means some kind of fight. Nobody does them willingly."

Does Mrs. Harris realize the price she's paid for getting chores done? Two daughters making every effort to separate themselves from her, three younger children who could easily be doing the same as early as possible?

"Life means responsibility," Mrs. Harris protests. "How else do you teach them?"

Life and being a parent also mean closeness and caring. What a parent wants to encourage in the parent-child relationship is love. Nobody loves his top sergeant; forced "responsibility" is a sentence, not a sharing of the tasks that keep a home running smoothly.

PETS AND RESPONSIBILITY

Another form of "teaching responsibility" that's common and probably as equally unproductive as lists of chores is "Get the child a pet and that will teach him to be responsible." I wonder how many puppies and kittens end up being the total responsibility of Mother as soon as the novelty wears off. Who feeds the pet, walks it, cleans up after it? And what has become of the lesson in responsibility it was supposed to teach? A child who doesn't take pride in being responsible because such behavior is approved isn't going to become responsible because he suddenly has a dog to take care of, just as a child who's friendless isn't going to make friends just by being sent to camp and put in touch with a lot of other kids.

"Responsible" behavior is the product of praise and encouragement for being grown-up, for acting in ways that show independence. In other words, simply putting the dirty clothes in the washing machine isn't anything more than a mechanical action, but the parent's recognition that helping with the washing and praising the effort makes the chore worthwhile, and a source of self-pride. Helping when you're needed is grown-up; the specific task is unimportant, but too many parents see the task done or undone before they see what it represents.

The way to teach responsibility is, I think, a matter of seeing the small but valuable actions all children do from time to time that are "grown-up" and then giving those actions positive recognition so that the child will repeat it, or something similar—because "being grown-up" brings parental approval.

Sharon has gone a few houses down the street to play with a friend. Before she left, her mother said, "Be home by five o'clock, Sharon," and Sharon promises that she will be.

She's home promptly at five. Wisely, although it was expected behavior, her mother praises the six-year-old for doing what she had promised.

"It was responsible of you to come home on time," her mother says. "I like to see you doing that."

The little pieces of the whole picture of being grown-up and responsible are put together as Sharon gets older. She takes good telephone messages; that's grown-up. She volunteers to help set the table. It may be simply a question of imitating what Mother does, but it's a job grown-ups have to do, so her mother praises her for helping—and when, in the future, Mother asks Sharon to set the table, it's not a chore that *has* to be done, it's the grown-up thing to do. In years to come, when Sharon is a teen-ager going out in the evening and she's told to be home at a certain hour, it's mature and responsible for her to do so, not a requirement that is there to be circumvented if she can.

"Clean up your room, how can you stand this mess?"

For some kids, cleaning up isn't all that important.

"I don't want to."

"Well, I want you to, and you have half an hour to do it. Grown-ups have to clean up after themselves."

Somehow it doesn't make being grown-up so valuable—being responsible for having an orderly room or a bed that's made first thing in the morning, if it's put in these terms. On the other hand, a parent who doesn't make the neat room or the made bed an issue between parent and child isn't going to suffer the strain of constant disputes. "You will" and "No I won't" are about as far as the argument should go, lest the appeal of a lot of attention over the messy room, or whatever the chore in question, overshadows either the benefits of getting it done or the parent's satisfaction in being obeyed.

The fact is, a parent's words are heard; the child knows that the chore under discussion is something that the parent wants, and one day the room gets cleaned up beautifully, with all the toys and books in their proper places. Now is the time for praise, for communicating values, for making the connection between doing a chore and what's grown-up and responsible.

"You did a terrific job cleaning up your room. It pleases me to see you taking care of your things. . . . That's very grown-up."

There are a lot of myths about how to teach values, and the one that does a good deal of harm to the relationship between parents and children is that work, obeying orders, will make a child into a responsible adult. Unfortunately it's one of those magic formulas for behavior that just doesn't work. It extracts a high price in many cases because of the opposition it can create.

Praise builds responsibility, and, to praise, you must see and encourage the quiet behaviors that are responsible behaviors in miniature. Lists and assignments aren't enough, not if the price you pay is a weakening of the bonds of caring between you and your child.

12

It's Grown-up to Be a Caring Person

"I want Alison to grow up to be a happy person who cares about other people as much as she cares about herself. It seems to me that both things are terribly important."

Alison's mother is right. One of the least-stressed, most-overlooked qualities of maturity is genuine sensitivity and caring for others. We hear a lot, maybe too much, in the media about "sensitivity" and "emotional bonds" and the like for people who have suddenly discovered that they don't have it (or think they don't). People who develop the techniques have a field day with the subject, because it's so abstract that it can mean whatever they want it to. It can give rise to opportunities for "talking it out," and hours of therapy to set emotions free, and "getting in touch" with your feelings and the feelings of others. It has become a lucrative occupation for the variety of advisers who claim to guide men and women to learn how to be sensitive. Sometimes these forms of therapy work, and often they don't. No parents, though, want to admit that this is what the future holds for their children—a sense of emotional incapacity that has to be corrected. They want, like Alison's mother, to have their children acquire a sense of caring as part of the process of growing up. What they don't realize is that the caring behavior they're talking about is a kind of positive behavior that is teachable at a young age, and that is related to all the other behaviors we have been talking about.

A caring child or adult has friends.

He has a good self-image; he knows he does things that others think are worthwhile, and therefore he is worthwhile.

A responsible child or adult cares about the effect of his actions on other people. They, in turn, trust him.

Part of responsible behavior is being aware of one's actions in relation to others, sensitivity about how a certain kind of behavior is going to affect another person.

The bonds of love between parents and children that flourish in an atmosphere of praise, in environments that feel good, are extended in later years to friends, to spouses, to children.

The rate of divorce in this country is now approaching 50 percent, and how many times are the grounds something like incompatibility or cruelty or irreconcilable differences, phrases of the law that very often simply define a lack of caring and sensitivity, the fact that people often find it difficult to show (or even to feel) genuine bonds of affection for others. Even when a husband and wife, for example, do "care," they may never have learned how to give and take, how to see caring behavior when it's being shown—just as some parents cannot "see" quiet behavior in their children.

In our world it is far too common to view things negatively, the kind of negative scanning that makes parents see only what is not right and ignore what is. We are back again at the theory that focuses on the disease, the problem, instead of on what is healthy and problem-free.

You can teach your children caring behavior, and you can take a child who seems to have little sense of what caring about others means and give him or her a foundation for happiness that is perhaps one of the most significant aspects of being "grown-up."

WHAT IS CARING BEHAVIOR?

The things that signify caring in our society are different for different people. Very often between adults, married couples, for example, caring behavior can be a lot of small things they do for each other. In fact, Dr. Richard Stuart, who works with couples who have marital problems, has a system of "caring days" where couples make an effort to build a good, caring relationship by doing just those little things that signify caring to each spouse.

We can build this attribute of adulthood in our children by teaching them to be caring when they are young. It's a matter of creating in them that positive feeling of self-worth so that they are easily able to build the self-worth of others.

We call it "thoughtfulness," an important caring behavior that has wide implications in the grown-up world, where the response to thoughtful, caring behavior is close bonds between friends and associates, between spouses, and with one's children.

"Isn't that cute," we say of children who do something thoughtful spontaneously. But it's more than cute, and we should be heavily praising the child who calls a sick friend to see how he is or tells another that he's really sorry he can't come over but be sure to call again tomorrow. Sharing is thoughtful, a gesture like picking flowers for Mother or all the little things children do that show they are not just thinking of themselves but are sensitive to the feelings and needs of others. Sibling caring, which we spoke of earlier, is a natural bond, but it is the parent whose eyes see this and other caring behaviors and who encourages them.

We teach children with praise, with labeling the many different actions as valuable. It's part of the job of being a parent, whether or not you yourself are especially caring and thoughtful, to teach your children what it means. It's a lot less expensive than raising children who don't know how to care and end up as adults who search for answers about how to make people like them, how to express what they feel for others.

Rick's teacher noticed his lack of sensitivity for the feelings of his classmates in the fifth grade. In an attempt to be funny, he would say things like "You look like a monkey," or "You can only play backstop" to a heavy boy during a recess baseball game. If the other kids laugh at his insensitive comments, he gains a slight feeling of self-worth. When he finds fault with other children, he also increases his feelings of self-worth at the expense of others—by making someone look inferior, so that Rick feels superior.

Rick's parents, and his teacher on occasion, have tried to change Rick's behavior, to make him more sensitive to the feelings of others.

"We've reasoned with him. We've asked him how he would feel if the shoe were on the other foot and people said those kind of things about him. We've asked him time and time again why he says these things. Nothing does any good. It's as if he doesn't hear us, he only hears those kind of embarrassed laughs he gets from the other kids."

Those laughs are a distorted form of "praise" for Rick, even if the kids themselves are slightly uncomfortable about it. His insensitivity results in people paying attention to him.

The way to teach Rick more sensitive behavior is not to talk about it, because the criticism implied by recounting what Rick has done wrong ensures that he's not listening. It's the nonteachable moment, and more effective in teaching Rick is a brief, immediate reprimand: "I don't like what I hear. I don't want you to talk that way to anyone." He knows, without discussion, that his behavior isn't appropriate.

The process for teaching more sensitive behavior is the same as previously outlined: praise, communication of values in the teachable moment following praise, and an extra reward in terms of enjoyable time. Praise for the smallest incidents that show sensitivity, whether or not Rick really feels caring: a moment of sharing, a comment that builds up another child rather than tearing him down, a gesture that shows Rick is thinking of the other person.

In teaching that caring behavior we help build self-esteem, and if a child feels good about himself, he'll find it easy to care about how his friends feel. Caring is the kind of behavior that reaches out years into the future.

Parents can teach caring by recognizing it and making it as valuable to the child as it is to them. It is an important lesson in becoming grown-up, and the ability to reach out and respond to others with sensitivity and understanding is something the youngest child can begin to develop so that it is a positive behavior that lasts for a lifetime.

13

Learning to Learn

A child with difficulties at school gets a lot of attention, not only from parents but also from teachers and classmates, administrators and counselors.

For parents especially, failure in the academic area and behavioral problems at school loom very large: what happens to the child, whether or not he or she learns what's being taught, is related to what the future will be, chances for higher education, the choice of jobs, the ability to compete in the world as an adult.

Recently, too, we have been handed a great deal of information and speculation about learning problems—those of the so-called learning-disabled child, the hyperactive child, even the gifted child—and how to "cure" them, which implies again that children's behavior has as its source a "problem" somewhere deep inside. Educators and psychologists often devote their careers to finding and exorcising the "demons" that seem to be hindering the learning process.

But learning, or a lack of it, is a behavior like any other, and positive learning-related behaviors, from wanting to or being able to read to paying attention in the classroom, are ways of acting that a child is taught. Parents have as much responsibility to encourage and nourish thirst-for-learning behaviors as they do a sense of responsibility, making-friends behavior, and all the others we have discussed. Once again, they must clear away the obstructing idea that a child who has difficulties in school is burdened with a demon or neurological deficit that is holding him back or causing him to be disruptive in the classrom or makes him resist going to school, and focus clearly on exactly what the behavior is, how it can be discouraged, and how a thirst for learning can be encouraged.

SMALL BEGINNINGS

Where does a thirst for learning come from? What makes a child like to learn, want to read? So much of what a child learns derives from his ability to read, even nowadays when electronic communication of information and entertainment seems to dominate. Whatever the future may bring, the knowledge we acquire still comes largely from the printed word rather than from electronics. The inability to read well is at the bottom of most learning difficulties.

Parents are often heard to say, "She never stops talking," or "We can hardly shut him up." Not too many say, "That child never stops reading." Talking, of course, is fun and it gets an immediate response. While many children do find reading "fun," it seldom gets a similar response from the world around them, certainly not in the same immediate way and often not until long after the habit of reading is well established.

The truth is that the consequences of learning to speak words and the consequences of learning to read are quite different. These two kinds of learned behavior are given different responses by parents. Just learning to say "Mama" provokes a lot of attention, hugs, smiles, encouragement to say it again, to say new words. The day a child of four or five first figures out what those black squiggles on a page mean is not the same kind of red-letter day in most households. There are few immediate consequences. In fact, the major consequences come somewhat later, when people start paying attention because a child cannot read, or doesn't like to learn in school, or won't pay attention possibly because he or she has never been sufficiently praised or encouraged for reading and learning.

"But we read all the time," a parent will say. "There are books all over the house."

Imitation, as has been mentioned, is not a reliable way to encourage behavior. Teaching by example, communicating the value of learning simply by being a learning-oriented parent, may not have much effect on a child. The best it can do is to give a little extra encouragement.

On the other hand, parents can do for learning—and we are really speaking of the most fundamental learning skill, reading—what we do in the normal course of growing up for speaking (immediate positive consequences). They can give a child a thirst for learning before he reaches the highly complex process of formal education.

It must be pointed out that there is a distinction between teaching behaviors such as responsibility, being a better friend, being independent and grown-up, and teaching thirst-for-learning behaviors. A winning-friends behavior, for example, is relatively isolated. It exists (or doesn't) within comparatively narrow limits, and while a lack of friends may have an effect on the child's life, parents can encourage or discourage actions within that class of behavior without too much difficulty. When we speak of formal education, however, we are dealing with a structure of learning that has certain prerequisites if a child is to make progress. Reading and math are taught step-by-step, and if the child misses out on a step, he can't successfully go on to the next. Parents can't do this, however much "help" they want to give with homework. Formal education, in the long run, must be in the hands of professionals.

However, the basis for a thirst for learning rests with the parents, who can make it worthwhile—set the stage, as it were, for the formal process that begins when a child enters school.

PUTTING HONEY ON THE LETTERS

The tradition of learning the Hebrew alphabet gives us an expressive image of how parents can instill a thirst for learning early by giving rewards for such behavior. Jewish boys in the Middle Ages were given slates with the Hebrew alphabet written on them, each letter coated with honey. The boy licked off the honey and learned the letters—learning was made "sweet" in a concrete fashion.

We already make speaking "sweet" by rewarding it. The parent who wishes to instill an eagerness to learn in a child must remember that reading must also be made "sweet" with encouragement.

Praise for making sense out of the black marks on a page in a book—"That means *cat!*"—deserves as much attention as that first spoken word, "Mama." The value of being able to understand what words written down mean has to be communicated, and *not* when the child is already in the midst of a school situation but during preschool years. Being able to identify a few letters seems insignificant, but teaching this essential tool of education is, I think, the one way parents have of giving a child a taste of honey and the sweetness of learning.

So many learning problems arise because a child sees no value in reading; there are few rewards in the early years, and when the time comes when "rewards" are granted by grades on papers, the child who doesn't do well is likely to be burdened with a label that defines his learning abilities for all time to come. In short, high value must be placed early on the behaviors that school will reward—the honey has to be there.

THE "LEARNING-DISABLED" CHILD

"Joey isn't learning in school, he's not achieving," his parents say. "He's in the fourth grade, and we don't think he's made any progress at all since he's been going to school. He's always been an active child, and he doesn't concentrate well, so he doesn't pay attention, and he doesn't learn.

"Of course," they add, "we knew when he first started school that he had a problem. His nursery school teacher told us so, five years ago. . . ."

The nursery school teacher, faced with an active boy who, while seemingly quite bright, didn't make an effort to learn, decided that "Joey is learning-disabled. Something is causing him not to learn like the other children. He has a problem."

Joey can't learn because he's learning-disabled. He's learning-disabled . . . because he doesn't learn.

The "why" of one is answered by the "why" of the other, whereas the reality is more likely to be that Joey hasn't *learned* to learn, so he doesn't learn. He is labeled as "learning-disabled," which means only that he has learned *not* to learn.

By the fourth grade his parents and teachers are frustrated.

"He knows something one day in arithmetic and the next day, or two days later, it's as if he's never heard of it before. He'll learn his spelling words and then almost at once he forgets them. Nothing stays with him."

"He's very unhappy," his mother says. "He

has what I'd call a poor self-image, no confidence in himself. He calls himself a dummy, yet we've had neurological examinations and all kinds of tests that don't seem to prove anything. But he's had trouble ever since he started school."

Does his mother spend a lot of time with him to help him with schoolwork?

"Oh yes. We read together and work on homework. In fact, he'll remind me that he has homework so I should allow time to help him. But I feel I have to help him, because he has this problem of being learning-disabled."

How does she know?

"They told us, and we can see for ourselves that he's getting nowhere. I know if he does something just a little bit well, he's so much happier. If I can do anything to help him, I have to."

Joey has a problem. It's her responsibility as a parent to do what she can to help him, even though no one is able to explain to her how it can be solved. How, indeed, can it be solved, if it's true that there is some undetectable defect in Joey's brain that has "disabled" him? But the only evidence of this is that he doesn't learn, he forgets things, he thinks of himself as a "dummy," he has no confidence in his abilities or himself. Just what is causing the problem?

CAN A LABEL CAUSE A PROBLEM?

At the age of four or so, Joey was given a label that has stuck with him through his school years.

Sometimes children are labeled as shy or uncooperative or spoiled and, as we pointed out earlier, children have no way of checking up on abstract labels. They believe what they hear. "Learning-disabled" may not be quite so easily grasped but the effects of the label are that Mother and Father and teachers know what it means, and they are in a position to see learning behavior that confirms the label and respond to it. They pay attention to the negative behavior and allow the quiet moments, when Joey is learning or showing learning behavior that could be encouraged, to pass unnoticed. Joey has been labeled a special child with special needs; parents and teachers redouble their efforts when they see evidence of his "problem" and give him special treatment.

Mother sets aside time to help with his homework; his teacher puts him in reading groups with other children who have been labeled as having "problems." There is a great deal of parental involvement, and there is far less encouragement for Joey to break out of the behavioral pattern that's been set. It doesn't take long for the whole situation to become a self-fulfilling prophecy: by the fourth grade, Joey is indeed "learning-disabled." The behavior he *has* learned is not to learn. And along with the payoff for having learning problems, parental involvement, there's a big negative payoff. He's getting left further behind (and has been heard to remark, "I'm *only* in the fourth grade. My mother kept me back a year"). His poor self-image is going to last him a lifetime. To educators and psychologists, labeling a behavior seems to explain what is happening, while, of course, it does nothing of the kind. A boy or girl who is having trouble in school is called "learning-disabled," as if that enabled us to understand the problem. It is an illusion; we know nothing more after the label was given than before. At best, labels are worthless in a practical sense; at worst, they are destructive.

"Learning-disabled" tells us nothing more than that the child is having problems with learning. Neither the label, nor the neurologists who try to determine whether there is "minimal brain damage," nor the educators who test ability to learn, nor the psychologists who try to uncover the emotional causes for learning problems can offer effective solutions.

One theory of learning disabilities really has to do with behavior and consequences. The honey wasn't put on the letters. Reading, and other kinds of learning behaviors, received minimum immediate rewards. Is it possible now to reverse lack of learning behaviors, in the way we can work on defiant behavior or no-friends behavior?

I don't want to suggest that parents of a child who has fallen behind his classmates in school because of variously diagnosed learning difficulties are going to be able, single-handedly, to change learning behavior. In the first place, so much of the difficulty takes place in the school environment where parents have less influence, and there are many more people involved than in the home. I do suggest, however, that parents of young children who are labeled as learning-disabled (or one of the other labels educators use to describe children with learning problems) examine the child's behavior carefully in the terms we've been discussing before they simply accept the label as reality and then assume that labeling is a step toward a solution.

In spite of the many theories put forward about the cause of learning disability, there is no "cure," except, it seems to me, in focusing on the behavior and how it developed. There are ways for parents to decrease the encouragement given at home for school problems of this type, but unlike the situation with other behavioral difficulties, one cannot give any firm assurances.

To go back to Joey, who has learned to be learning-disabled, perhaps initially he didn't get encouragement for thirst-for-learning behaviors, praise for quiet moments when he first discovered letters or numbers. When his nursery school teacher decided he must be learning-disabled, because he couldn't learn even though he had average or above-average intelligence, the problem began to affect not only Joey's ideas about himself but those of his parents and his future teachers. He received attention for not learning.

His parents were able to make a small beginning toward helping him out of his problem. They tried to make the label less significant by decreasing their attention, constant help, and visible concern. At the same time, any indication of positive learning behavior that filtered through to them (even the reading of a newspaper headline or spending time with a comic book) received praise.

Joey's mother remembers that he came home excited and happy because for that day he had been put in a higher reading group—an opportunity for praise and some rewarding time spent with her. Even a page of homework completed or a neatly written paper (the spelling mistakes don't cancel out the effort) could be turned into an occasion for making Joey feel a little more worthwhile and able to learn.

In the final analysis, however, the burden of working with children who have been labeled learning-disabled, like the whole process of formal education, has to lie with the professionals. Only a professional can actually "teach" a child the steps of learning in a formal environment to help him catch up and, one hopes, make learning a rewarding experience. Whether the professionals are truly able to bring the child up to grade level is doubtful in most cases, and this makes it tremendously important for parents of preschool children to sweeten the interest in learning as early as possible, even though the ultimate rewards are distant.

THE HYPERACTIVE CHILD AND OTHER PROBLEMS

I remember meeting with a teacher about a boy in her class who had been having learning problems. He, too, had been labeled "learning-disabled" because he wasn't learning. He was disruptive in the classroom, talking out loud and refusing to stay in his seat, disturbing the other children and making life miserable for the teacher, even though she'd been told about the boy's so-called problem.

She told me, "You know, if I didn't know that Carl had a problem, I would say that he was obnoxious." The label required her to overlook the obvious about Carl; something in our problem-oriented society had persuaded this teacher, and countless other teachers and parents, to view the Carls of the classroom not as badly behaved children but as children driven by a problem. If a child is behaving in an obnoxious manner, there is one set of consequences—certainly, at least, trying to put a stop to it. If the same kind of behavior has an appropriate label, "learning disability," it has an entirely different set of consequences attached. The behavior that should justifiably make a parent or teacher angry, for example, becomes a behavior that requires solicitous concern, attention, special help: in short, all the kinds of response to behavior that *encourage* its continuation.

Hyperactivity is a current favorite among educators and psychologists, as well as medical people who are trying to pin down the "cause." The evidence that has been gathered about chemical additives to food, allergies, and nutritional deficiencies as contributing factors to hyperactivity doesn't do much about the actual behavior: how inappropriate behavior has been made worthwhile to a child, why it continues, how it can be reversed.

Some children are more physically active than others, some have shorter attention spans, some have had so little encouragement to read and enjoy learning that thirst-for-learning behavior is no part of their behavioral repertoire and hence no classroom situation can hold their interest. The more unpleasant learning becomes, the more they act to escape.

"She's hyperactive," an educator or psychologist will say, and indeed the child in question is less interested in sitting still and paying attention. The label has been applied, and forever after, the behavior is going to be encouraged by the attention that is paid whenever "hyperactivity" manifests itself.

Melissa has learned that a certain kind of behavior, which the grown-ups in charge of her label as hyperactivity, will make her the center of concern at home and in the classroom.

"What did you do when her teacher told you Melissa was hyperactive?"

"Our very first thought was 'We've got a problem,'" parents will say. They will find out what they can about hyperactivity to file away in a convenient pigeonhole.

Suddenly they have a problem child with no answers guaranteed to solve his difficulties.

But there may be an answer, and it has to do with the behavior that is being inadvertently rewarded. The parent (and the teacher) disturbed by signs of "hyperactivity"—whatever cause may be uncovered eventually—is going to pay attention, and thus make it behavior that is encouraged.

183

The same pattern can be seen with children who have so-called dyslexia, or who have minor speech problems. A young child learning to read or to speak stumbles over words or writes a letter backwards. Parents are immediately concerned; they look for more instances. The label is applied, and time and attention are centered on the problem. There is an immediate payoff for writing letters in the reverse direction or stuttering. It should be remembered that *even if* it is possible to determine some physiological or neurological cause for the difficulties we have been discussing, the repeated additional attention and involvement given such children may inadvertently encourage the behavior. It encourages its existence, helps it to grow, teaches the child that it is worthwhile to see letters backwards, to stutter, to disrupt home and classroom with excess activity. What has to be encouraged are not noisy behaviors but those that indicate just the opposite.

DIANE LEARNS INDEPENDENCE

Fortunately, many kinds of school difficulties do manage to avoid getting labeled with the name of a popular "problem," and it is largely a matter of seeing what is going on objectively and then encouraging the right kind of behavior. The case of the boy discussed earlier who didn't take pride in his schoolwork, forgot his gloves on the playground, and couldn't manage to finish his papers is a "school" problem, but it was solved by his parents' making achievement in school and grown-up attention to his belongings and work valuable behaviors.

Diane, for example, was reported by her second-grade teacher to be unable to work independently.

"She works slowly at assigned tasks, although when I sit beside her and encourage her, she often does the task quickly and easily," her teacher said.

At times, Diane appeared to be unsure of herself, spoke in a shy, soft voice, and asked her teacher and friends to do things she should be able to do herself, like zipping up a zipper or putting her boots on.

"There's no question that Diane's a bright child," her teacher said. "She can do the work and she understands things well. The problem seems to lie in her unwillingness to do things on her own. She's not assertive, she'd rather rely on others. When she's supposed to be working on her own, she invariably looks to me or her classmates."

Luckily, Diane's teacher took an objective look at her and didn't take the easy route of deciding that Diane needed psychological testing to uncover some sort of problem. Diane simply needed to be able to take the intelligence and capability she obviously had and turn them to good account by learning to be more independent and to have more confidence in the person she was.

In talking with her parents, it was clear that they catered to her quite a bit, and they admitted that since she was the youngest child, they and her older brothers and sister encouraged her to be dependent at home. They helped her with her clothes and gave her plenty of opportunities to let them do things that she should do for herself.

When she went out into the wider world of school, however, behavior that was a matter of course at home was viewed in a different way by teachers and fellow students; her lack of independence had a negative effect on her learning. In a class with many children making demands on a teacher's time, Diane's dependence on others, if only to confirm that she was doing worthwhile work, was unacceptable.

By putting the two viewpoints of Diane's behavior together, her teacher and her parents were able to see her difficulties clearly and to follow a system of praise and reward for grown-up, independent, responsible behaviors (at home, doing things without her parents' or brothers' and sister's help; at school, doing her assigned work without the teacher at her side). At the same time, the time devoted to her immediately following "working slowly" or "not-working" behaviors, or other less grown-up kinds of behavior, was kept to a minimum. There was no longer a payoff for being dependent, and Diane's so-called learning problems became a thing of the past.

The point with school problems, from school phobia (not wanting to go to school at all) to behavior that disturbs an entire classroom, is to look at what is really going on. Again, "understanding" a child is less profitable in changing behavior than seeing the reality: what a child actually does and what kind of rewards are given for the behavior to make it worthwhile.

The many teachers I work with have found that the system of praise and reward is highly effective, and it quickly becomes part of their whole philosophy of dealing with all the children in a class.

"When I get angry at the end of a rough day as I see Tom whispering across the aisle or Cathy bullying one of the other kids about something, I take a step back and remember that screaming isn't going to do anything but make Tom or Cathy the center of attention. I leave it at a reprimand, and try the next day to find something in Tom or Cathy to praise. It saves wear and tear on me, and it makes the kids a little bit more proud of themselves and what they can do."

14

The Question of Discipline

A leading advice-giving columnist advises an anxious parent to send a naughty child to his room for thirty minutes as punishment. It supposedly gives the child time to contemplate his misdeeds and see the error of his ways (so the parents hope). It is doubtful, however, that a half an hour, usually in a room filled with toys, will make the "punished" behavior occur less often. In fact, the only positive benefit (for the parent) would seem to be that the child is out of sight for thirty minutes.

The question of discipline and punishment—for there are certainly occasions when they are necessary—is a difficult one. It doesn't follow that if praise builds positive behaviors, some form of punishment stops negative ones, especially if the "punishment" takes the form of "a good talking to"—the very kind of attention that centers on the child, giving him parental time and concern. On the other hand, true punishment in terms of a total absence of rewards can be highly effective if it is used sparingly. In addition, it should be used only for serious misdeeds, for example, cursing parents, hitting parents, and intentional destruction of objects.

The best punishment is one that is infrequent.

The best punishment is immediate.

The best punishment is brief.

PUNISHMENT AND PARENTS

"I was punished as a child. I never like to punish anybody. I don't like it."

This mother has a child who very much needs to have limits clearly set. Roger does do a lot of things that are serious, that have to be stopped when they occur, yet his mother admits that her method of dealing with serious behaviors is ineffectual.

He is consistently disobedient. He gets to his mother by saying, "You hate me. What kind of mother are you?" He hits his mother, he curses her. He hits other children.

"I just can't seem to punish him, but I'm building up a resentment toward him. I see mothers who say, 'Stop doing that,' and just with the tone of their voice the kids stop. They say, 'I don't like that, don't do it,' and the child doesn't do it anymore. If I say 'Don't do that' to Roger, he does it one more time. He doesn't stop misbehaving."

Roger and his mother, because of her inability to put a halt to the behaviors that trouble her, face repeated battles that only create increasing feelings of resentment and anger between parent and child.

"I've seen mothers take one look at their child, and that does it. The child knows he's doing something wrong and stops . . . just one word stops them."

If Roger's mother wants her "looks" to be effective, that "one word" has to be associated with a meaningful consequence. The consequence can be many things: no attention whatsoever, a reprimand, or a form of stronger punishment. The words must initially be followed by immediate punishment, in order to make them meaningful.

"I DON'T WANT TO TALK ABOUT IT. . . ."

Throughout this book, we have dealt with how to encourage positive behaviors with praise and rewards, and how to take a close look at children with behavioral problems to see how they have been given unintended encouragement.

When Cindy eggs on her parents with comments like "You don't love me, you hate me," they rush to reassure her that they certainly do love her. Their inevitable response is her reward; she has their attention, they give her their time. As has been pointed out, taking away these rewards makes the behavior less worthwhile. The absence of a reward is a punishment, and for most behavioral problems a simple "I don't want to discuss it" is an effective non-reward that acknowledges the behavior and expresses disapproval.

Completely ignoring a behavior is not effective. If parents say nothing at all, the child is likely to increase the shock value of the behavior until he or she *does* get a response. Behavior must be acknowledged, but it should not be followed by long reasoning sessions or reprimands.

"I DON'T WANT YOU TO DO THAT. . . ."

Another step in non-reward that acknowledges a behavior and expresses disapproval is a brief, angry reprimand. Brevity is important, a firm resistance to being drawn into a discussion about the behavior.

Eddie is a problem at mealtimes, banging his fork on the table, kicking the table leg, dominating the meal with complaints and refusal to eat. Even as his parents have learned to give encouragement to the moments when he shows good mealtime behaviors, he still continues those irritating bad behaviors. The response to them has to be, not the long-drawn-out arguments that have occurred in the past, but a short angry comment: "I don't want you to do that" or "Eddie! Do not bang your fork."

I have found that this sort of reprimand, replacing a good deal of attention, changes the feel of the environment effectively, and while the good behavior builds, the negative behavior tends to diminish, since rewards are minimized for negative behavior except for the few words that express strong disapproval.

TIME-OUT

Sometimes more forceful punishment is necessary, but parents must remember that the best form of punishment is that which is used infrequently and, when it is, is *immediate* and *brief*.

The most effective punishment is one that denies a child access to people, to the environment, to the many satisfactions in his world (for that reason, thirty minutes in his room is useless, since there are a multitude of satisfactions in his room—television, trains, toys).

For the most severe kinds of misbehavior, the best punishment is time-out, a near-total absence of rewards for five minutes. It is equivalent in part to the old-fashioned schoolroom method of sitting a child in a corner.

Following are the recommendations for punishing extremely disruptive behaviors that I gave the parents of five-year-old Delia, which show clearly how punishment ought to be handled (other recommendations, of course, showed the parents how to encourage a positive class of behaviors).

I. When Delia engages in extremely disruptive behaviors:
   Kicking someone,
   Cursing Mother or Father,
   Having temper tantrums,
   Hitting Mother or Father . . .

II. *Immediately* tell her, "We do *not* . . . (kick, curse, scream, etc.)."

III. *Quickly* take her by the hand (*say nothing*) and seat her in a small chair on the first floor facing a *blank wall*. If Delia screams or kicks while in the chair, ignore her. If she leaves the chair, be near enough so you can *quickly* (without saying a word) return her to the chair (avoid a chase).

If she pleads that she will be good, ignore her.

Don't talk to her, don't tell her to be quiet.

IV. Delia must remain in the chair for a minimum of five minutes. If at the end of the five minutes she has been quiet during the last fifteen seconds, quickly go to her, praise her, tell her she has been quiet and well behaved, and she may now leave the chair.

V. If, at the end of five minutes, Delia is kicking or screaming or even talking, she must remain in the chair until she has been quiet for 5 to 10 seconds. As soon as she has been quiet for this time, quickly go to her and tell her she has been quiet and well behaved and that she may now leave the chair.

VI. Never allow Delia to leave the chair while she is misbehaving, and do not discuss the punishment afterward.

The judicious use of time-out is probably the best way a parent can discipline a child. The taking away of privileges for long periods of time (days, weeks, months) encourages deep feelings of resentment toward parents.

This time-out method of punishment will be effective if it is used infrequently and for behaviors worth punishing—for the most serious behaviors only. (Even 99 percent warmth and affection and 1 percent punishment is too high on the punishment end of the scale.) Any form of punishment used too frequently and for minimal cause stirs up anger and resentment toward parents and gradually destroys the bonds of affection between parents and child. When it is an immediate response to an extreme behavior, it can, if properly used, eliminate that behavior.

15

Building for the Future

Thoughtful and considerate children mean happy children and happy parents. Life is easier if there are few problems. But what is the point of building a repertoire of appropriate behaviors beyond having a childhood that is free of excessive anxieties for parents and full of satisfactions for children?

After the first dozen years of life, there's a long, long time from adolescence to old age. The foundation for those years is laid in the first years, when the group of behaviors that we might call the personality of the individual is learned with guidance of our parents.

Parents are concerned about the problems and perils of adolescence, when the influence of peers becomes all-important. It's far more difficult then to direct a young person to the people and activities we think are right, if we haven't established these basic behaviors in the child.

However, the child who makes friends easily, for example, at six or eight or ten, who draws people to him because he has a sense of humor, is thoughtful, caring, interesting, is likely as a teen-ager to attract the best of his contemporaries—and want to be with the best of them. The kids who hang around on street corners, get into trouble, find that drugs and alcohol give them the illusion of being "grown-up," are not the children who have been taught genuine grown-up, responsible behavior. Those children who do know probably have positive feelings of self-worth that were nurtured with praise from their early years.

If being home on time is considered grown-up in a ten-year-old, it will be thought so by the sixteen-year-old. If answering the telephone and taking a good message is a way of being responsible in someone who's six or seven, the seventeen-year-old is going to know without thinking that he is responsible for fulfilling those obligations. If a small child respects the feelings and property of others because it's a caring behavior that is grown-up, the boy or girl in the teenage years is going to behave in the same way. Thoughtfulness in children means thoughtful adults, happy marriages where husband and wife don't need a program of caring days to show how they feel. Thoughtful adults mean parents who will in turn teach thoughtfulness to their children. Children who have been taught thirst-for-learning behaviors will become adults who don't stop learning, even though they are finished with their formal schooling.

Raising happy children means creating the conditions for happy adults, who find the satisfactions of life within their grasp instead of always eluding them.

One mother said to me recently when discussing her son's behavioral problems, "What do I want for him? I just want him to be happy." It's what we all want for our children, and the way to happy children is to give them the behaviors that mean happiness and create feelings of self-worth that last a lifetime: being a good friend, knowing the satisfactions of responsibility, having an eagerness to seek out knowledge, and possessing a sense of caring.

Appendix: Recommendations; Classes of Behavior

The method of changing a child's behavior that I teach parents can be applied without the assistance of a psychologist. For the parents who do come to me for help, I provide a series of recommendations they can refer to that relate to the specific problem behavior they are concerned with.

Following are several such recommendations, as they were written for individual children, to guide you in seeing how the method is formulated, and how it can be used.

RECOMMENDATIONS: JUDY (ELEVEN)— FRIENDS/SCHOOL

At the present time, Judy appears to be doing somewhat better in terms of her relationships with her classmates. One description of her relationships with other children is "She gets along all right, but there are no in-depth friendships."

In order to put Judy more in touch with her classmates, both at school and outside of school, it might be helpful to encourage those behaviors that will make her classmates want to be with her and seek her out as a friend.

I. *To encourage behaviors that will make others seek Judy out as a friend.* Examples you might note:

1. Shares pens, pencils, etc. (sharing).

2. Takes turns during game (thinking of others).

3. Laughed at Carol's joke (sense of humor).

4. Told a girl she likes her sweater (praise for others).

5. Thanked a classmate (politeness).

6. Asked other students about their vacation plans (interest in others).

7. Gave appropriate gift (thinking of others).

8. Helped with a math problem (helpfulness).

9. Interesting conversations (turning on people).

When noting these behaviors, *be specific:* what did Judy say, what did she do? Note two to three examples each week.

Note these behaviors:

even if they are brief,

even if they are ordinary,

even if they are expected behaviors,

even if she does them all the time,

no matter what the motivation,

no matter what happened before or what happens afterward.

We are looking for ordinary, not necessarily extraordinary, examples of these behaviors.

II. *When you observe these behaviors, on occasion:*

1. Note specifically what she said/did.

2. At a later-time (one to six hours later) and at your convenience, take her aside and attempt to make that earlier situation come to life again by describing it vividly. Tell her what she did, what she said, and with whom.

3. Then immediately praise Judy. Tell her this behavior pleases you.

4. *Then quickly tell her what the behavior means to you:* e.g., "You were being a good friend. People like that in a friend."

5. Then (once or twice during the week), you might *immediately* and *casually* follow the praise by spending five to ten minutes with her talking about something she enjoys, or by suggesting an activity you know she likes ("How would you like to . . . ?") Do this as though the

idea had just occurred to you at that moment. DO NOT say, "Because you have done such and such, I will allow you to do this or that."

III. *Reminders must be specific*

Telling Judy she "played nicely" or seemed to get along with Johnny when they were playing this morning is unlikely to encourage good peer-relationship behaviors. It does not tell the child what behaviors went into the making of the good relationship such as the sharing of some object, or the listening to what the other child had to say.

IV. *The teachable moment*

The teachable moment occurs immediately following words of praise. If you want to communicate values and ideals that are important to you, it is best to communicate them immediately following praise for behaviors that represent even small examples of those values: e.g., honesty; how to relate better to one's age mates ("that's the kind of thing people like in a friend").

RECOMMENDATIONS: PAUL (FIVE)—EATING

I. *Suppertime*

1. If Paul (a) stuffs food into his mouth or (b) gulps the food down quickly, make a

very real effort not to lecture him on the virtues of good eating habits. Don't tell him not to stuff his mouth or to eat more slowly.

If you must comment on these behaviors, make it brief, and do it infrequently. Say something like "No, Paul," with a stern look on your face. *If possible, say nothing.*

2. If a piece of food slips off Paul's plate, there should be no comment about this. You can't expect perfect table manners from a five-year-old. Repeatedly telling him what he is doing wrong at the dinner table will not improve his table manners. It will only associate eating with unpleasantness.

3. If Paul does not eat all the food on his plate for a particular meal, he should not be forced to finish the meal. He may leave the table without dessert.

    a. Wrap the plate in food wrap and put it in the refrigerator. *Don't coax him to return to the table.*

    b. Anytime before bed, Paul may ask for the meal he didn't finish. He may have it from the refrigerator as it is—*cold.* If the meal is finished, or nearly finished, he may have dessert.

II. *To encourage good eating habits*

1. Take note of Paul when he is doing things

205

at the dinner table that you would like to see more often:

a. Eating properly with his fork and spoon.
b. Eating more slowly.
c. Asking to have food passed.
d. Eating a nonpreferred food (even a small amount).

2. Briefly tell him what he is doing *at the time it is occurring*. Don't say, "I am proud of you, you aren't stuffing your mouth." (This doesn't tell him what he is doing right.) Don't say, "You are eating so nicely." (This also doesn't tell him what he is doing.)

Tell him *specifically* what he is doing ("You are eating more slowly," "You are cutting your food so well," "You are using a napkin").

Then praise him: "That was grown-up."

III. *After the meal*

1. On occasion, take Paul aside, tell him specifically what he did at mealtime that pleased you, and *make your words bring the situation alive again.*

2. Praise him.

3. Then *immediately* and *casually* follow the praise by spending several minutes with Paul doing something he likes to do, as though the idea to do this came to mind at that moment.

RECOMMENDATIONS: MIKE (SIX)— DISRUPTIVE BEHAVIOR (FOR APPROXIMATE AGES THREE TO NINE)

Examples of Mike's disruptive behavior, such as pushing a child, throwing rocks, hitting a child, represent inappropriate expressions of angry feelings. We do not want Mike to hold his anger in. Rather, we want to teach him more appropriate ways to express his angry feelings and eventually work toward teaching him social skills which will make the events that lead to anger occur less often.

There is a tendency to view angry outbursts as a way station toward appropriate assertive behaviors. As such, one often mistakenly encourages these behaviors.

1. Violent behaviors and assertive behaviors are *two separate classes of behavior;* one does not lead to the other. Violent behaviors are *not* a prerequisite for assertive behaviors.

2. If one encourages violent aggressive behaviors, this type of response to frustration will more likely occur in the future.

I. *When disruptive, violent behaviors occur*

1. Immediately tell Mike, "We do not hit/ push, etc."

2. Quickly take him by the hand to the chair facing a blank wall, and seat him there.

3. Mike must remain on the chair for a minimum of three minutes.

4. If he turns around or tries to leave the chair, quickly return him to the chair. *Say nothing to him at this time.* If he screams or kicks ignore him.

5. If at the end of three minutes he has been quiet for the final 5 to 10 seconds, quickly tell him he has been quiet/well behaved, and may now leave the chair.

6. If at the end of three minutes, he is kicking, or even talking, he must remain in the chair until he has been quiet for ten seconds. Then *quickly* tell him that he has been quiet/well behaved and may now leave the chair.

7. Mike must never be allowed to leave the chair while he is misbehaving.

8. Do not discuss the punishment *afterward*. Long discussions of this type teach the child that negative behavior is rewarded with total parental involvement.

II. *To teach Mike more appropriate ways of expressing angry feelings*

1. When Mike expresses his anger in a violent manner, don't divert his attention to punching bags or knocking down blocks. Don't try to teach him to "let out" the anger in these ways. *This will simply teach him to be more angry.*

2. Instead, it is more appropriate to provide Mike with the model of a person who is relaxed in the face of minor problems. For example, if Mike spills something and is very upset and angry, you might say, "It's okay, Mike. We'll get a sponge and clean it up." This provides him with a model of a relaxed attitude, and also a technique for solving the minor problem.

3. If an upsetting event occurs—e.g., a child takes a toy from Mike—his old response might be to push the child. We wish to teach Mike a new response to the event, assuming he has reason to be upset because a real injustice has occurred. Tell Mike how he might have responded: e.g., tell the child, "Don't take my toy." What we want to do is to teach Mike how to speak up, how to be appropriately assertive, *how to express his feelings of anger in an appropriate manner*. To do this, simply tell him how he might have behaved under those frustrating circumstances. (We call this a *prompt*.)

4. If he imitates the prompt, either immediately or at a later time:
   a. Tell him what you observed (be specific).
   b. Praise him (100 percent praise).
   c. Tell him why his behavior is valued, i.e., it indicates that he is mature, more grown-up, more a big boy.

    d. Quickly follow the praise with five or ten minutes of a favored activity.

    e. If you are praising him at a later time, be sure to remind him of his earlier behavior as vividly and specifically as possible.

This punishment is for extremely serious behaviors only. You should not be using this method more than one or two times a week after the first week (if the method is being used properly).

RECOMMENDATIONS: BARRY (SIX)— DEFIANCE

Barry is at times defiant. On occasion, nothing will make him do what he doesn't want to do. At nursery school, he refused to do a paper, refused to color and, unless it was something he felt he wanted to do, he wouldn't do it.

Barry's defiance may be viewed as his way of asserting his independence. His behaviors may be saying, "I am a big boy; you can not tell me what to do. I am grown-up and I will make my own decisions." When his mother lays out his clothes and he says, "I don't want to wear those shoes," this is his way of saying, "You may lay out my clothing before school, but I have the final decision on the shoes."

This is a very healthy striving. We surely would like to encourage Barry's wish to do more things on his own and to be more grown-up, responsible, and independent. However, Barry has learned some inappropriate ways of expressing this wish to be more grown-up and responsible. What he needs to learn are appropriate ways to prove he is grown-up . . . ways which will make him feel good about himself as a more independent boy RATHER THAN ways which may be viewed as "phony expressions of independence." (Being defiant does not mean you are grown-up/independent).

The more Barry feels grown-up/independent for behaviors which truly indicate that he is responsible and grown-up for his age, *the less* he will have to be defiant to prove he is grown-up.

I. *To encourage grown-up, responsible, independent behaviors*

Examples:

1. Cuts his own meat, using knife.

2. Brings laundry basket up from basement.

3. Poured his own milk.

4. Walked to bus stop on his own.

5. Made his own lunch . . . bologna, cheese, bread.

6. Changed from school to play clothes. Came out all changed and said, "I didn't want to get my school clothes dirty." *Responsible Behavior.*

7. Dresses self/matches clothing.

8. Answers phone in a grown-up manner. NOTE HOW.

9. Any on-his-own behaviors.
   Be Specific. What did he do/say that was grown-up?

Note 3–4 examples weekly even if they are brief, even if they are ordinary, even if Barry does them all the time.

Note them no matter what the motivation is, no matter what happened before or happens afterwards.

When *you observe* these behaviors . . .

A. *At the time of the behavior . . .*

1. Try to *clearly remember* what Barry did and said that was responsible, grown-up.

B. *At a later time (1–4 hours later and at your convenience) . . .*

1. Take Barry aside and, as *vividly* as you know how, remind him of what he did earlier that day. Using words, attempt to make that earlier behavior *come to life again. Do not say,* "You were very grown-up this morning." Tell him what he did, vividly, that indicated to you he was grown-up.

2. Praise him . . . tell him how pleased this made you feel. 100% praise only with no mention of any less grown-up behaviors of the past. *Do not say,* "It's nice to see that you poured your milk

without spilling it all over the floor, Barry." *Do not say,* "You poured your milk without spilling it, *for a change.*"

3. *Immediately* follow this by briefly telling Barry what the behavior MEANS to you . . . grown-up/responsible/big boy.

4. *Immediately* follow this by spending 5-10 minutes with Barry doing something, or talking about something which he enjoys, as if the idea had just popped into your head, i.e., "How would you like to play ball?" or "Let's go out and have some ice cream." *Do not say,* "Because you were so grown-up I will spend 10 minutes with you." Just do it as though it just occurred to you following the praise, telling him what the behavior meant to you.

THE SEARCH FOR SELF-ESTEEM BUILDING BEHAVIORS

Low Self-Esteem Behaviors	Self-Esteem Building Behaviors
A. Immature behaviors	MATURE, RESPONSIBLE BEHAVIORS
B. Defiant behaviors	MATURE, RESPONSIBLE BEHAVIORS

| C. Turning off friends behaviors | HOW TO WIN FRIENDS BEHAVIORS |
| D. Non-motivated behaviors | A THIRST FOR KNOWLEDGE BEHAVIORS |

As a first step, attempt to determine which low self-esteem behaviors best describe your child. Ask yourself what he is doing, what he is saying that to you reflects your major area of concern . . . are they behaviors in categories A, B, C, or D (Choose one category)? To help you arrive at this decision, *briefly* jot down specific examples of those behaviors which are of major concern to you. Note 3–4 examples on a separate sheet of paper. Spend no more than 5–10 minutes noting negative behaviors, AND NEVER DO THIS AGAIN. Be specific. Note what your child does, what he says, that to you indicates defiance, immaturity, a lack of motivation or behaviors which are responsible for his not having friends.

Then begin looking for the opposite class of behavior, the appropriate self-esteem building behavior (i.e., Turning Off Friends Behaviors—look for How to Win Friends Behaviors).

No matter how immature a child is, no matter how defiant he is, no matter how often he is antagonistic toward other children his age, there are within his behavioral repertoire the beginnings of, THE OPPOSITE OF THESE BEHAVIORS . . . which if encouraged, will help increase his feelings of self-worth.

Since these behaviors are "behaviors in miniature," they are ordinary rather than extraordinary SELF-ESTEEM BUILDING BEHAVIORS.

II. Note specific examples of these behaviors (see examples from "classes of behavior" listing on page 216).

DON'T WRITE, "HE WAS RESPONSIBLE," rather, note what he did do/say that indicated he was responsible.

DON'T WRITE, "HE PLAYED WELL FOR 30 MINUTES. . . ."
Note what he did and what he said, that in part made for the play activity go well, as well as the friend's behavior.

CLASSES OF BEHAVIOR

The *specific kinds of behavior* we want to encourage are represented by *small actions*. Parents often need direction to help them see examples of behavior in the class that need the push of praise to help the behaviors grow. The child who is not responsible, is babyish, and consistently behaves that way still does things from time to time that are responsible and mature.

Following are some lists of specific behaviors in the three major classes. Parents are reminded to remember *specific details* of the behavior (what was said, who was present, what was done) so that in describing the scene later, it can be brought to life again for the child.

Responsible, Grown-up Behavior

1. Picks up toys after playing.

2. Gets dressed on his own.

3. Listens during story hour at the library.

4. Speaks in a grown-up manner (note how, what is said).

5. Makes breakfast for parents (eggs and toast).

6. Takes a phone message well (note how).

7. Takes key to school and lets herself and little sister into the house after school.

8. Feeds the cat.

9. Changes promptly from school to play clothes.

10. Is home exactly on time.

11. Makes Jell-O on his own.

12. Brushes her own hair well.

13. Packs his own snack, does it well (note how).

14. Orders at a restaurant in a grown-up way (note how).

15. Is patient waiting in a line with parents.

Making-Friends Behavior

1. Takes turns in a game.

2. Shows an interest in what another child says (asks questions that indicate he is listening).

3. Good sense of humor, which makes other children laugh (note what was said).

4. Is polite, saying please and thank you.

5. Shares toys.

6. Praises a friend for doing something well.

7. Allows the other child the choice of activity (opposite of being bossy).

8. Asks friend to come back again tomorrow.

9. Calls friend who is sick to see how she is.

10. Has interesting play ideas (note ideas).

11. Greets everyone at school in a friendly way (note how).

12. Compliments a friend on the way she looks (note what was said).

Thirst-for-Learning Behavior

1. Any kind of reading—newspapers, books, comics, even headlines or words in a TV commercial.

2. Reading signs on a trip.

3. Using long sentences to describe something.

4. Following directions.

5. Writing neat, interesting letter to thank a relative for a gift.

6. Reading a story aloud to a younger brother.

7. Counting money.

8. Seeking additional information by using an encyclopedia or creative behaviors (note specific behaviors).

Index